Alexander. [from old catalog] McLean

Food for the Lambs

Alexander. [from old catalog] McLean

Food for the Lambs

ISBN/EAN: 9783744646581

Printed in Europe, USA, Canada, Australia, Japan

Cover: Foto ©Andreas Hilbeck / pixelio.de

More available books at **www.hansebooks.com**

FOOD FOR THE LAMBS:

OR,

SERMONS FOR CHILDREN.

BY

REV. ALEXANDER McLEAN,

OF BUFFALO, N. Y.

" Feed My Lambs."

NEW YORK:

N. TIBBALS & CO.,

No. 37 PARK ROW.

1868.

CONTENTS.

The Shepherd and His Lambs.

Isaiah xl. 11. "He shall gather the lambs with His arms, and carry them in His bosom."

IT is almost spring, children — almost spring. Cold winter will soon be gone. The sun, when it gets a chance to show itself through the clouds, seems to laugh, as if it were saying to itself: "I will soon melt the icy fetters upon the little brooks, and make them dance along to their own music. I will soon change the bare brown fields into green meadows, and make the flowers which have been so long buried peep forth. I will soon chase away the dark clouds which now hide my face, and call the poor, sick child from his bed, to enjoy my

A 3

warmth, and those who are in health, to enjoy
my light." Yes, spring-time is coming. In
a few weeks it will be here, in all its glory.
Opening its lap, it will strew the earth with
verdure, flowers and blossoms; and with its
sweet voice, call upon all to praise the Lord
for His goodness, who sendeth us the seasons
at the appointed time.

But I think I see some of these little girls
looking at me with wondering eyes, as if they
would like to ask what this has to do with my
text; for children know just as well as grown-
up people, that a sermon should be all about
the text, and there is not the first thing said
about spring here.

Let us read it again and see. "He shall
gather the lambs with His arms, and carry
them in His bosom." Not a single word
about spring, you see. But let me ask you
when do you see the lambs? Not in cold
winter, when the ground is covered with
snow, and the frosty winds whistle around our
dwellings. They come, like the birds, with
the flowers. You would laugh at a painter
who should make a picture of winter—every

thing white with snow—and should add to it
lambs, gamboling in the snow-covered fields.
You would say at once that he had made a
mistake—that if he wished to make lambs, he
should paint green fields, bright with sunshine. This is right. Now, children, I think
that our text is a very beautiful picture of
spring: a picture not made of colors, but of
words: a picture not seen by the eye, but by
the mind. I know that children love pictures. Come, then, and look at this one with
me. It is the picture of a far-off country—a
beautiful country. It has high mountains
and wide valleys. It has springs and fountains of water, shaded by cool palm-trees.
How green the pastures look; how pretty are
the roses of Sharon, and those sweet lilies of
the valley. How much brighter and bluer
the sky is than ours. Those white, fleecy
clouds which are chasing each other, appear
so pure, that they might be mistaken for the
downy wings of infant angels, at play. Now
I think I can hear the sound of music—simple
music, but sweet, as if a shepherd was near,
piping upon his reed. And so it is. Yonder

is his flock, resting in the shade, while he is resting under the majestic palm-tree. The sheep are resting, but the lambs, like a troop of merry children, are playing, as if the day was too short for their sports. You can see that the shepherd is good and kind, for those lambs, so tender and timid, are not afraid of him. One tiny lamb, a wee, weak thing, is sleeping on his bosom.

This is the picture which we have in the text; is it not a beautiful one? If I could I would paint it so that you could look upon it whenever you chose; so that, by looking upon the picture, you would always think of this text. For I consider it one of the most sweet and precious in the whole Bible. If I can only make you understand and love it, I know that it will not only make you wiser, but also happier, all the rest of your life. For then you would be able to say, like that little shepherd boy, who became a great king: "The Lord is *my* Shepherd, I shall not want." You need not wait till you are grown up, for this —for the Shepherd that is spoken of here, has lambs as well as sheep in His great flock.

Indeed He does not mention the sheep at all here, only the *lambs*. And by the lambs are meant the little ones—children, no matter how young they may be. This then is really a text for children, and surely if there are texts for children in the Bible, there should be sermons for children, so simple that they can understand them.

I wish you to remember, then, that this is *your text*—to remember it, after you have forgotten all that I may say about it, in trying to make it plain. I like to give my sermons a name ; I will tell you what I have called this : "The Shepherd and His Lambs." From what I have said already, you know that I am not going to talk to you about flocks and herds— nor yet about Abraham, who was a shepherd —nor Jacob with his smooth hands and soft voice—nor yet about the shepherd boy, who killed the lion and the bear, when they came to steal his sheep—nor even about those shep- herds who were watching their flocks by night, whom the angels told that the Saviour was born. This might be interesting to you. But the Shepherd I will tell tell you about is

A5

a still more interesting subject. And that you may remember what I shall say, I will divide it into three parts. First I will tell you—

I. Who the Good Shepherd is, and why He calls himself by this name. Secondly—

II. Who are His lambs, and why He calls them by that name. And thirdly—

III. How kindly He cares for them.

First, then, I am to tell you—

I. Who is the Good Shepherd, and why He calls Himself by this name.

I see that Charlie wishes to answer, "I know, sir, it is Christ; for He said, I am the Good Shepherd." But Janie there, knows that the whole Bible was not written at once, and looks as if she wanted to tell me, that it could not be Christ, because He had not come into the world, when Isaiah was the prophet of the Lord. Now it is true that this verse was written six hundred and ninety years before the shepherds on the plains of Bethlehem were told by the angels, that Christ was born. Many years before Christ came, Isaiah died, and his body had become dust, in the

tomb of his fathers. And some of you may
ask, How could he know any thing about
Christ? If you look in your Bibles, you will
see, that the part of it, in which the text is
found, is called, "The book of the prophet
Isaiah." But what is a prophet? If I could
tell you, where every one of you would be,
and what you would be doing, ten or twenty
years hence, I would be a prophet. But who
can do this, unless God tells them? No one,
not even the wisest man that ever lived.
Why children, we cannot tell even what shall
be on the morrow, much less what shall be
ten, twenty, or a hundred years after this.
All we know is, that before a hundred years
shall pass away, we shall all be sleeping in
our graves, and other children shall fill your
places, who neither know nor care any thing
about us. Perhaps they may go to the grave-
yard where we are sleeping, look at the
stones, which have become black by years,
and try to spell out our names. Or they may
look into the book, which contains your
names, when the ink has become pale, and the
paper yellow with age, and merely say, See,

here are the names of the children, who came
to this Sabbath school, a hundred years ago.

But Isaiah could tell a great many things
which were to come to pass after he was
dead. Why? Because God told him, and
made him write them in a book, and it is
from this book, more than two thousand years
old, that we have read the text. And it has
all come to pass, just as he wrote it. When
we read some parts of his book, it seems, as if
he must have lived in the days of Christ. He
tells about His wonderful birth, and how the
wicked Jews would treat Him. He speaks
about His sufferings and death, as if he had
been one of the disciples who watched with
Him in the garden, and beheld His suffering
upon the cross. And then to think that he
could say, "He shall gather the lambs with
His arms, and carry them in His bosom," just
as if he had heard Christ say, "Suffer the little children to come unto me, and forbid them
not, for of such is the kingdom of heaven."
So, Charlie, you are right when you say that
Jesus is the Good Shepherd. I need not stop
to ask you who He was. You have been too

well taught, both at home, and in the Sabbath
School, to need to be told this. The youngest
of you can tell me all about the holy child
Jesus. What I wish to explain to you, at
this time, is, why Christ calls Himself the
Good Shepherd. And first—

1. As a shepherd knows every lamb in his
flock, so Christ knows all the children.

There was a man who travelled in Palestine
—the land in which Jesus was born—who has
told us that he saw a shepherd, watching over
his flock. To the man, the lambs looked all
alike. He could hardly tell one from another.
But the shepherd knew them, every one; and
could call them all by their names, and as he
called them they would come to him. Now,
children, this is the way with Christ. He
knows every one of you. For although He is
now in Heaven, yet His all-seeing eye is upon
earth. He knows you, and can call you all
by name. This is very wonderful indeed; I
wish we all thought about it, far more than
we do. The Good Shepherd knows you, just
as well as if you were the only lamb in His
flock. Your name is written in His book.

When, therefore, you read, "I am the Good
Shepherd," remember, children, that He calls
Himself by this name, that you may know
and feel, that He is acquainted with you.
But again :

2. As a shepherd watches over his flock,
and takes care of them, so Christ watches
over and takes care of you.

You know that it is the duty of a shepherd
to feed his flock, to lead them in green pastures, beside the still waters. He must see
that there is something for every lamb ; not
one of them must suffer. Now, it is just in
this way that Christ has been taking care of
us. He has supplied all your wants. We are
all apt to forget, when we sit down to the
table, spread with God's mercies, that it is
just as much furnished by Christ, as if He
came to us, morning, noon and night, with
the food which we need, or sent a raven to
feed us, as he did the prophet, at the brook
Kedron. And if we can but say, The Lord is
my Shepherd, we may also add, I shall not
want. When you grow older, you will find,
children, that a great many are very much

troubled about what they shall eat, and what
they shall drink, and wherewithal the shall
be clothed. But if you are Christ's lambs,
you need never fear. You may say—He will
provide.

Let me tell you a story here, to show you
how Christ takes care of His own people.

Not many years ago, there was a very good
but very poor minister, thrown out of employ-
ment. The people did not want him to
preach for them any more, because he insisted
on telling them their duty. Soon, all that he
had in the world was gone, and yet he did
not fear but that something would be provided for him. The last meal that was in the
house was eaten. His children had for the
first time to go to bed supperless. It pained
him very much to hear their cries. What
could he do? Nothing but pray, spreading
before God his wants. Thus he spent the
whole night. The morning at last dawned.
He told his wife to spread the table for break-
fast, just as usual, and told her not to be
afraid—the Lord would provide for them, and
their little ones. Soon a knock was heard at

the door; they opened it, when a letter was handed to him, with these words, "From a friend." He opened it, and found that it contained ten dollars. Afterwards he learned that a gentleman in the neighborhood had passed his house that cold winter morning, and the thought came into his mind that the poor minister might be in want of fuel, and he went home and sent his servant with that welcome note.

Now, some would say, that this only *happened* so. But I would rather believe that this was the way which the Good Shepherd took, to supply the wants of one of His servants. If He could send the ravens to feed Elijah, why can we not believe that He put this thought into the heart of one of His servants? I tell you, children, if you wish to be happy in this world, you must become Christians, and then you need feel none of those fears which trouble other men. For as a shepherd feeds his flock, so does the Lord provide for the wants of all His lambs.

But another reason why Christ calls Himself the Good Shepherd:

3. Because He defends His lambs from all danger.

You know that lambs cannot defend themselves—the wolf might come and kill them : neither can we, for we are weak, timid things. But when Christ's arms are round about us, no danger can befall us. You have sometimes been afraid in a stormy night, when the winds were whistling around your dwellings, rattling the casements, and moaning as if there was a spirit in the storm. And you have begged your mother to sit by you, till you fell asleep. When she was near, you felt no danger. Now, although Christ is in heaven, His arms are around all His children. When you say, "Now I lay me down to sleep," committing yourself to His care, you may go to rest quietly, feeling that no evil can come nigh you. The wind may blow, but He holds it in His hands. The clouds may hide all the stars, but His eye sees you, through all the darkness. Oh, it is blessed to know that Christ calls Himself *our Shepherd*, for now we shall want for nothing, and need fear nothing. For Christ knows us all, and watches over us all, by day and by night. But now I must hasten to tell you in the second place:

II. Who are Christ's lambs, and why He calls them by this name.

It is a very important question for each of you, children, to ask yourselves, Am I one of Christ's lambs? Is He my Shepherd? And now I will tell you how you can know, and if you are not, how you can become a lamb in His flock. If you love Christ, and try to serve Him, then you are one of His lambs; but if you do not love and serve Him, you are not. I wish it was so that every child was one of Christ's lambs, but they are not, for only a very few of them truly love Him. They think that they have nothing to do with Christ till they grow old, but this is a sad mistake. They should all love Him now, and I will tell you how to begin.

You must go to Him in prayer, for you know He hears the prayers of children. And say to Him, "Dear Jesus, I am a weak and sinful child, but I would be one of the lambs of Thy flock. Teach me to love Thee, Thou

Good Shepherd, who didst say, 'Suffer the little children to come unto Me, and forbid them not.' Blot out my sins with Thy blood, and make me Thine." If you do this, in earnest, every day, He will say, You are Mine, I have taken you into My fold. He will not speak this into your ear, but into your heart, and you will feel it there. Now let me tell you some of the reasons why He calls good children His lambs. And first:

1. Because He loves them very much.

You have heard a mother call her child a little lamb. And you knew what she meant—that she was only saying how much she loved her darling. Now, Christ calls the children whom He loves His lambs, because they are so dear to Him. Why, children, He shed His blood for you. You have read the story of His sufferings—how he left heaven, and came to earth, and suffered and died upon the cross. But did you ever feel that He did all this for you? It was for you He suffered—for you He died. I wish you would read that chapter which tells us all about the sufferings of Christ, and at every verse say to yourself, All

this was for me, He so loved me, and then
you will know why Christ calls you His lambs.
He laid down His life for you.

But again, Christ calls good children His
lambs because :

2. They are so prone to wander away from
Him. Lambs, you know, are apt to wander
away, but they do not know how to find their
way back. A dog will find its way home,
although you should take it off a great many
miles, while a lamb would never find its way
back. And in this respect, children are very
much like lambs.

Said a little boy to his mother, " O, dear,
there is no use trying to be good ; before I
know it, I am doing something naughty, so
that I am afraid that I shall never be a good
boy." But his mother said, " Try again, and not
only try, but ask Christ to keep you good."
And, children, this is the only way. I knew
a man who was wicked, but wished to do better. He made a great many good resolutions
—he would not swear any more, he would not
get into a passion any more—but soon he forgot his good resolutions, and was just as wick-

ed as ever. But at last he became a Christian, and when he was tempted to do wrong, he looked to Christ for help, and became better and better, every day. Now, children, this is the only way that you can become really good. Look to Christ, as the Good Shepherd, for help. Say to Him, I am a poor little lamb, so ready to wander away from Thee—take me and guide me. And whenever you do wrong, cry to Him, I am straying from Thee, keep me for Thy mercy's sake. But again :

3. Children are like lambs because they cannot defend themselves.

You know that the lion in some countries, often attacks the tender lambs, seizes them and carries them off as his prey ; poor things, they can do nothing to save themselves. The Bible tells us of a roaring lion, who goeth about seeking whom he may devour. That lion is the wicked one. Now, if you had to defend yourself, you would surely be overcome by him. But the Good Shepherd stands and defends you. He says to Satan, "Touch them not— they are Mine, My arm is round about them ;"

and Satan leaves you. He cannot harm you
when you are Christ's. But now I have to tell
you in the third place :

III. How Christ gathers His lambs with
His arms, and carries them in His bosom.

You know, children, that there is such a
thing as death in this world. The body becomes cold and motionless, and although we
love it ever so much, we are glad to bury it
in the cold ground, out of our sight. But
you know, also, that we have souls as well as
bodies, and the soul cannot die. Where does
it go when it leaves the body? I will tell
you what we are told in the Word of God
about it. The soul goes to the fold of Christ,
and that is heaven. It is there that He gathers them with His arms. O, what hosts of
children are there. Around the throne of
God, on high, thousands of children stand.
But you know there is a very dark valley between us and that glorious fold. It is called
the valley of the shadow of death. And down
into that dark valley the Good Shepherd
comes to meet us. Father, mother, brothers,
sisters, cannot go with us there. But Christ

comes to meet His little lambs, and He takes them in His bosom, and carries them safely through, and then away up to His glorious home. There He leads them and feeds them, forever more.

Let me tell you about a little lamb that belonged to Christ's fold. His name was Willie. He was a sweet, pretty child, too good for this cold, dark world. He was always asking to be told stories about the angels. One day, when a good lady was talking to him about them, he said, "I should like to go to the angels." A few days after this he was taken sick, and the fever was so high that he was sometimes delirious. But he would often call out, "Dear mama, I am going to the angels." One pleasant afternoon he called his father and mother to his bedside, and said, "Good-by, good-by, I am going to the angels." His mother took his hand, and said, "Dear Willie, stay with us." But he smiled sweetly, and said, "The angels call me, good-by," and fell asleep, never to waken upon earth. It was another lamb gathered to the Saviour's fold.

O, who does not desire to have Christ for their Shepherd? Who does not wish to be one of His lambs? And then, after a few short years in this world, to be borne in His bosom to Heaven.

Good and Bad Words.

PROVERBS xxv. 11. "A word fitly spoken, is like apples of gold in pictures of silver."

I DO not know any thing in this world that sounds quite so sweetly as the praises of God, when sung by children. It is sweeter melody than the songs of the feathered tribes, even when in grand concert, just at the dawn of morning, they hail the return of spring. It is sweeter melody than the rippling of waters, as they dance along to their own music, throwing back the sunbeams from their ripples. Because neither the birds of the air, nor all the brooks, which like silver threads woven together, make the great rivers, know whose praises they are chanting in ceaseless song, while children know it is God, their Maker, whom they praise.

I wonder if there are any children who do not love to sing, or who cannot learn to sing? Yes, there are, and I would like to introduce you to some of them, to-day. Would you like to visit a school with me—a Sabbath School—where there is no noise, where not a single word is spoken from the opening to the close, where they never have any singing, and even when they pray, not one word is spoken? It is to such a school I would take you now. There is one such school in almost all our large cities. Here is one, in that great brick building. Can you read those big letters up there, carved in stone?—"Home for Deaf Mutes." Come up this flight of stairs—here is the door, marked "School Room."

But, hark! you do not hear any noise, no, not a single whisper. Perhaps it is not their hour for school. Let us open the door, and look in. Why, what a company of children! Count them—one hundred, one hundred and fifty, two hundred, two hundred and thirty-five. A large school, and how attentive they are. Not one of them has turned round to look, when the door was opened; there has not even been a single sly glance. Let me tell you the reason. These children have never heard a sound, and never will. They have never lisped a single word, and they never will, unless Jesus should unloose their tongues. They are the children of silence, or you will perhaps understand me better, if I call them the deaf and dumb. They cannot talk, they cannot hear you when you speak to them.

This is very sad, children, for there are thousands of these poor, unfortunate ones, in our country. Just think of that little blue-eyed girl, with hair almost like a sunbeam, beautiful as a picture, who never lisped that sweet word *mother*, and never heard a mother's voice saying, *my child*. Think of that bright-looking boy, with laughter in his eyes, whose face tells so plainly of all the emotions of his soul, and yet his dumb lips never said, my father, his deaf ears never heard a father's or mother's voice saying, my son. They never could tell of a want, they never could make a request, in words. When sad, they can weep, but cannot tell the cause of their grief. When happy, they can smile, but no peals of merry laughter can break from their lips, nor can they tell in words, the cause of their gladness.

But why have I commenced this sermon by telling you about deaf and dumb children. Read the text again, and you may perhaps be able to guess. "A word fitly spoken, is like apples of gold in *pictures of silver*"—or rather, in a basket of silver. That is, it is a very beautiful thing to see a nicely-carved basket of polished silver, filled with golden apples; and a word fitly spoken, that is, a good word, spoken at the right time, is just as beautiful as that, and as precious, too. We can all speak. God has not sealed our lips as He has the lips of those poor mutes that I have told you about. And I hope you will all thank God to-day for the gift of speech.

There is one advantage which deaf and dumb boys and girls have, and that is, they have never spoken and never heard, a wicked word.

The wise man has told us what a good werd is like, but who can tell us what even one wicked word resembles. I cannot. It is such a horrible, monstrous thing, that I cannot find any thing to compare with it. Our lips were made to praise God, and I wish to show you to-day, that it is a great and good gift which He has given us—the gift of speech—that is, the power to talk. We can improve it, and by improving it, do much good; we can abuse it, and by abusing it, do much evil.

I will be very plain and simple, so that none of you will be able to say, when you go home, I could not understand the sermon. I will not confine myself to the text; if I did I could only speak about good words, for I have something to say about *bad words*, also. This will be a sermon on the use of the tongue; perhaps it will be plainer to say, on good and bad words. I will tell you first, about

I. Good words, and how beautiful they are.

Let us see if we can tell what a word is. It seems to be a very simple thing, *a word*—it

is a sound, and nothing more. But it is far
more than an articulate sound. Take one
word, *God*, and you see that these three letters spell the name of the greatest and best
Being in the whole universe.

Take another word—Jesus. When we hear
that word, we all know that it means that
great and glorious Being, who came into the
world to die for sinners, and who now lives
in heaven, at God's right hand.

Take another word—mother. That is no
empty sound. It stands for the one whom
you love, or should love, the best in the whole
world. She it was who watched over you
with such unceasing care, in sickness and in
health. That word mother, will awaken
sweet memories in your hearts, when they begin to grow cold and hard. At the mention
of that name you will be children again, and
live over the long forgotten past.

There is so much, then, in a *word*, although
it is only a sound which is gone as quickly as
it is uttered. The power to utter words, and
really know what they mean, is one of the
noblest gifts which God has bestowed upon

man. To use words well, gives any man an exalted position in this world. We call such an one an orator, and crowds flock to hear him speak. By words he can move them to tears or laughter, make them glad or sad, at his will.

One little insignificant man, with shaven crown, and coarse monk's dress, with nothing but words, did more than kings or emperors could do. He raised armies, through all Europe, and sent them to fight battles in a distant land. His name was Peter the Hermit.

Do you understand now, what words are, and the power which they have over us. They are not empty sounds, but the embodiment of our thoughts.

You think, but I cannot tell what your thoughts are, till you put them in words, then your thoughts are not your own any longer; they belong to me as well as to you.

A great many years ago, when people wished to send secret messages, they wrote them on paper with invisible ink. The person who received them held the paper to the fire, and what looked a few moments before like

sheet of white paper, was soon a letter, cover
ed with words. Now your thoughts, before
they are expressed in words, are to me and
every body else, like that sheet of paper before it was held to the fire, *invisible,* but as
soon as they are spoken, they are like the
words on the paper; after they have been
brought out by the heat, we can know them.

But another thing about words; when once
they are spoken, they can never be recalled.

In one of the salt mines in Europe, deep
down under the earth, there is a lake which
no breath of air ever disturbs. It is smooth
as glass. Around it are clefts of crystalized
salt, formed by God into all sorts of fantastic
shapes. Go out in the small boat, which is
moored at the side, into the middle of this
lake. Whisper one word, and from every
cliff it comes back like thunder. You are
startled at hearing your own voice, as if a
thousand unseen beings were mimicing you.
And it takes a long time before the echo of
that whispered word dies out.

Now, we do not hear the words which we
speak, repeated in echoes, but nevertheless,

children, it is true, that a word once spoken, be it good or bad, echoes on through the world, forever and ever. You cannot stop it.

The words which I have spoken to-day, and which I am now speaking, will never die. They echo from the very dome of heaven, and in a few years, when I shall stand before the judgment-seat of Christ, although both you and I may have forgotten them, I will hear them as distinctly as if they were spoken at that moment, and I shall be happy or sorrowful according as they have been good or bad words.

But it is time that I told you about some of the kinds of good words which are so beautiful. And the first which I shall mention, are—

1. *Kind words.*

A young man was one Sabbath evening walking through the common of a great city. His face was bloated, and his clothes soiled. He was a pitiable looking object. Few would have cared to speak to him. For it was just as plain as it could be that he was a drunkard, and was fast going down to a drunkard's grave.

An old man was walking through the common, but not to idle away an hour of the holy time God has given us. He was intent on doing good, and had gone forth that calm Sabbath evening, to look up some poor outcast whom he might help. Chance—no, Providence brought these two together. Some *kind words* fell from the old man's lips. They sounded strangely to the poor drunkard. It was many years since he had heard such words, and they reached to his very heart. It was an easy matter for the old man, then, to persuade him to accompany him to the house of God, to hear a temperance lecture.

He went, and heard himself described. The downward course of him who tampers with the intoxicating cup was shown. The young man saw his danger, and that very night made the resolve that he would forsake it forever.

Years have passed away since that Sabbath. The old man has gone to his reward; but the young man is still living a life of usefulness. Through his instrumentality thousands have been saved from a drunkard's grave.

And he acknowledges that all that he has become, is due to the kind words spoken to him by that good old man. How easy it is to do good, when so much can be accomplished by speaking a kind word. Kind words cost nothing, and yet they are almost as rare in this sad world as precious stones. Kind words are good words. They are like apples of gold in pictures of silver. But again:

2. *Faithful words*, are good words.

I mean when some one comes and kindly tells you your faults, that his words are faithful. You may always be sure that such an one is your friend, while the man who laughs at your folly, is your enemy.

Now, children do not love to be told their faults, nor, for that matter, grown-up people either. We all wish to have just as good an opinion of ourselves as we can, and so, because it makes us feel unpleasantly, when one has told us some things that we have done, which were wrong, we forget their kindness and are apt to be angry with them. But let me assure you, children, that the best friend you can have in this world, is one who will kindly tell you when you do wrong, and help you to do right

A great many years ago there were two little ships launched upon a very long river. Each of them contained a little voyager. The river was the River of Life, and ran into the great Ocean of Eternity.

These little ones were to make the voyage, each one for himself. In this river there are a great many rocks which you cannot see. If one of these little boats strikes against one of these, it is not only badly bruised, but it becomes unmanagable, so that you cannot steer it straight. These rocks are called faults, and should be avoided.

Now there were sailing in ships just ahead of these little ones, two who were much older and who undertook to be their guides. One was faithful to his task. Whenever the little boat dashed against one of these rocks, his friend ahead told him of it, and told him how to avoid it in the future. Thus they sailed along pleasantly till the great ocean came in sight; peacefully they entered it, and soon found a haven in the land of Eternal Rest.

The other did not perform his duty to his little charge. When the little voyager struck one of these rocks, he told him it was nothing, and only laughed at him. And thus the little boat became unmanagable. Before it reached the ocean it was just like a log upon the water, driven hither and thither. To this day it is a tempest-tossed thing. Never will the little voyager find a resting place through all eternity.

Let me tell you this in plain words. The little boy or girl who has a kind friend to tell them their faults, will learn in time to overcome them, and at last reach the happy home in heaven. The boy or girl whose faults are not corrected by kind words, become worse and worse, and are lost at last.

Think much, then, children, of those who tell you your faults. Their words are faithful and good. But again :

3. Comforting words are good words.

This is a sad world, children; if you live a little longer you will find it to be so. A good part that man acts in life, who is always ready to speak a word of comfort to the sorrowful.

B

A little boy stood one day beside the grave
of his mother.   He was all alone in the world;
his last and only friend was sleeping in that
grave.   He did not know where to go or what
to do.   He thought that no one pitied the
poor orphan boy.   He stood leaning against
one of the monuments, wishing that he was
down there in the silent grave beside his
mother.

A good man had entered the place where
the dead lie sleeping, to meditate upon death
and eternity.   He saw the little boy, with the
big tears undried on his cheeks, and kindly
taking him by the hand, asked him the cause
of his sorrow.   "Mother's dead," said the little boy, "and they have put her in the cold
ground; I will never see her again.   I have
no mother, no home; I wish I could die."

"Little boy," said the man of God, "I knew
your mother, and I know where she has gone.
An angel from God has taken her to His own
home in heaven, and there she is waiting for
you."   And then he told him how to live, so
as to get to his mother when he died.

What a comfort it was to the little fellow.

Hope sparkled in his eyes. There was some thing to live for now. There was a brigh' star shining brightly over him, and whenevei he was sad and sorrowful he thought of hi? mother waiting for him in heaven.

That comforting word fixed his destiny for time and eternity. The little boy became a man. He was a son of consolation to many while he lived. He sleeps now beside his mother in the old grave-yard, under the yew tree, but his spirit has met her's long ago, in that house not made with hands, eternal in the heavens.

It is easy to speak such comforting words, and thus be a blessing to others. Such, then, are some of the words which Solomon says are like apples of gold in pictures of silver.

But now, I must say something about *bad words*, although children, I must confess that I do not like this part of the subject, and would pass it by did I not know that they are so very common. It is easier to speak a good than a bad word, and yet there are more bad words spoken than good. I will only mention a few of the kinds which are most common. The first are

1. Untrue words.

They are very mean and contemptible; besides they are very wicked. You have all heard of the little boy who would not tell a lie. I think that was the foundation of his greatness. When he became a man every body could trust him, and depend upon what he said. And so they entrusted to him this great nation. But a boy who does not speak the truth—who will trust him when he becomes a man?

I know that children are sometimes tempted to tell a falsehood, because they think that by so doing they can conceal some wrong which they have done. But this is a mistake. God knows it; the falsehood cannot hide it from Him. Just think of having every such wicked word repeated before the whole world in the Day of Judgment. Oh, how those who have spoken them will hide their heads for shame then; for all secret things will be revealed. Then again, there are

2. Envious words, which are also bad.

Some people can never bear to see any one prospering but themselves, and so they must show their envy by speaking evil of them. It is far more honorable to speak words of praise; and if we cannot conscientiously praise any one who is spoken of, then keep silence. A good rule, and it is a very old one, too, is, "Never say any thing about a person who is absent that you would not say before their face." If this rule was followed, there would be far less evil speaking, and far more good will among men.

But now I must mention the **very worst** kind of bad words:

3. Profane words.

It is needless for me to tell you how wicked such words are, for God has said, "Thou shalt not take My name in vain." To take the name of God in vain!—who can be guilty of such wickedness? You have all heard the name of God profaned. I must say that I never hear a profane oath but what I feel afraid. It seems as though God must avenge His own insulted honor. But He for the most part keeps back His hand from vengeance. Sometimes, it is true, He strikes the swearer dead, with an oath half uttered on his tongue. Never does a profane word sound so awful as from the lips of a child. Your tongues were given you that you might praise the Lord. Oh, do not use them for such a wicked purpose as profaning His holy name.

You see, then, children, that the gift of speech is indeed a noble gift. We can speak kind words, faithful words, and comforting words. But this gift can be perverted. The tongue that can praise the Lord may also profane His name. The lips that might speak a word in season to one who is heavy of heart, may speak an envious, malicious, unkind word, which will be like plunging a dagger into the heart.

You see, then, that there is need to pray as David did, "Set a watch, O Lord, before my mouth; keep the door of my lips."

Royal Children.

---◦•◦---

JUDGES viii. 18. "Each one resembled the children of a king."

FEW years ago, as some of you children may remember, a boy came from England to this country, to see what was to be seen in a land where there is no king.

He was attended by a great many servants, who were as respectful and attentive to him as if he was something more than a mortal. Wherever he went, great crowds assembled to see him. When it was known that he was to pass through certain streets, every window was thronged with people, anxious to get a look at him. He was invited

D4

nere and there and every where. Sums of
money which would have supported a dozen
missionaries for years, were spent to give him
an entertainment for a night.

Had you met that boy in the street you
would only have seen a fair-faced youth, at
whom you would never have turned to look
again.   Why did they make such a great ado
about that boy?   It was not for any particu-
lar regard they had for him, but because if he
lived for a few years he would be the king of
Great Britain.   And it was thought to be
such a great thing to have a real live prince
in this country, even on a visit, that it was
really astonishing how people who believe
that one man is just as good as another, if he
only behaves as well, should have been so carried away by one who was by birthright a
king.

No doubt a great many thought it was a
very fine thing to be the son of a king or
queen, when they could have such honors
paid them; and perhaps you think so, too
To be waited upon by the noble and great,
to have a kingdom for an inheritance—there

are very few in this world who would de-
-pi it.

Yet, children, I am going to tell you to-day
how you may all become the children of a
King, and have a crown and kingdom which
are more precious than if all the nations of
the earth could be formed into one kingdom,
and all the crowns of kings and potentates be
formed into one crown. If you could have
all these offered you, the crown and kingdom
which I have to offer you to-day, would be
worth far more than them all.

It is my great desire that you should all be
not merely like the children of a king, but
should be really king's children. It would
not do you much good to *resemble* the Prince
of Wales, but to *be* the Prince of Wales might
be a very fine thing. I will now tell you how
you may be the children of a King far greater
than any king you ever read about in history.

And first, let me tell you about

1. The King whose children you may become.

There is One, of whom we read in the Bible, who is called the King of kings, and

Lord of lords. You all know who that must be. It can be no other than God Himself. He says of Himself, I am a great God and a great King; the King of the whole universe; not of this little world of ours only, but of all the worlds which shine above us.

You have been out some clear, cold night, when there was not a single cloud to be seen in the sky. It was a deep blue, sprinkled all over with stars. It seemed as if they were almost crowding one upon the other in some places, and in others as if they were only a hand's breadth apart. They looked very small, too, as if they were no larger than good sized diamonds. But this is only because you are so far from them.

Some years ago I went with a friend to the top of one of the tallest steeples in New York. From the dizzy height we looked down upon the streets. It was a strange sight. The men looked like little boys, and the boys like infants. The streets seemed so narrow that you could step across them, and the houses any thing but like the great tall buildings they were. The reason was that we were so far above them

This is the reason that the stars look so small, because we are so far from them. They are millions and millions of miles from this world, and are really very great suns and very great worlds, and God is King over them all, for He made them all.

You know, children, there was a time when there were no worlds, no heavens, and no earth. There was only God—Jehovah—Father, Son and Holy Ghost. They said let us create, and by a single word They lighted up the heavens with suns, and scattered worlds all over space. By a word, They created angels and archangels, and last of all, man himself. And because God is the Creator of all, He is King over all.

A king, you know, must have a kingdom, a palace, and a throne. King Solomon dwelt in a palace of cedar, and had a throne overlaid with pure gold. All Judea was his kingdom, and the twelve tribes of Israel his subjects. His word was law to them; he had life and death in his hands.

But far greater is the King whose children you may become. The house with many mansions is His palace. Let me read you a description of it. "And the building of the wall of it was of jasper. And the city was pure gold, like unto clear glass. And the foundations of the wall of the city were garnished with all manner of precious stones. And the twelve gates were twelve pearls; every several gate was of one pearl. And the streets of the city were of pure gold." What a beautiful palace that must be—the home of the great King.

God has made this world very beautiful. He has hid gold under the mountains, and diamonds in secret places, and pearls in the depths of the sea. But upon His own palace He has lavished all wealth; every thing that is rich and rare, costly and grand, bright and beautiful, He has there.

Then that palace has a throne. It is so glorious that when angels approach it to worship, they cover their faces with their wings, and taking the jeweled crowns from their brows cast them in homage at the feet of Him who sitteth thereon. O what a great and glorious King God is!

That you may have a better idea of regal glory, let me tell you what power belongs to a king in eastern countries; and God, you know, has greater power than they, for He is King o: kings, and Lord of lords.

We will go to the palace of Sushan, and look at Queen Esther when she goes in to ask a favor from the king. She is a Jewess. The king has sent forth a decree that on a certain day, all her countrymen are to be put to death. She is going to beg for their lives, and her own. She is very beautiful, and her natural beauty is adorned with costly robes and glittering gems. She has every thing to make life attractive.

To go into the king's presence unbidden, is death. Yet she braves the danger, breathing a silent prayer to heaven, and "if I perish, I perish," upon her pale lips, she passes in, and how mute and pallid, yet calm and resolute, stands outside the ring of nobles who surround the king's throne, to hear her doom. The king may be angry, and it will be death to her. He may receive her graciously, spare her, and grant her petition.

Beside him is an iron and a golden sceptre If he raises the iron rod she will be instantly led forth to execution; if the golden sceptre, she can go boldly up the line of nobles and present her petition. Her suspense is of but short duration. The golden sceptre is extended to her. She hears the blessed words, " What wilt thou Queen Esther? and what is thy request? it shall be given thee, even to half the kingdom."

She asks favors for her oppressed countrymen, and the king is true to his royal word. Her requests are granted. Such is the reverence and awe in which earthly kings are held, and such is their great power.

But *our* King is still more to be revered. It was to His throne that we approached a few moments ago, when we addressed Him in prayer. It was a golden sceptre that he held out to us, and if we asked aright, He will hear and answer our prayers. Think of this every time you pray, that you approach the throne of Him who is the King of kings. A little child like you could not get into the presence of an earthly monarch to present a petition;

but God invites you to come into His very throne room, and there bowing before Him, to ask for whatever you need. You can ask nothing so great that He cannot give. You can ask nothing too small for Him to regard. Your every want can be supplied by this great King.

Would you not like to be His children; the children of God? Let me tell you then

2. How you may become His children.

This King, the great God, had a Son; a well-beloved Son. He lived with His Father through all eternity. He made this world; and we refused to obey and serve God, His Father. This was a very great sin, the sin of rebellion; for which we all deserved to die, and must assuredly have died had not the Son of God said, "I will save them." How do you think, children, He did this? You know God is a Spirit; He has not a body of flesh and blood, like ours. He is here, but we cannot see Him.

This reminds me of what a little boy said about a poor woman who came to his house not long ago. His mother asked him if he was not sorry for poor Sarah, she had no body in the world to love and care for her—she had to live all alone. "No, ma," said he, "she has somebody to care for her." "Yes, a Father in heaven," answered his mother. "No, but somebody *here;* she is not alone, for she has God to take care of her." That was all. true. God does take care of those who love Him, and He is ever with them, although we cannot see Him, because He has not a body, like ours.

What is true of God is also true respecting His Son. So that the first thing He had to do when He came to save us was, to take a body like ours. You know He became the babe in Bethlehem. That little infant sleeping in His mother's arms is the Son of God. That little boy, who goes up to the temple to worship, is the Son of God. That sorrowful man, who walks by night on the Sea of Galilee, when the waves are rising up like mountains, is the Son of God. That man who stands in Pilate's judgment hall, clothed in that tattered purple robe, with that crown of thorns upon his brow, is the Son of God.

That poor sufferer, hanging faint and bleeding upon the cross (O children do you not pity Him; for not only is He suffering in body, but His heart is breaking with sorrow), is the Son of God. He became all this to save you. It is for you that He is suffering, bleeding, dying, and He has sent me to ask you if you will have Him for your Saviour. You are a poor sinful child, but you can go to Him and say, "Lord Jesus, take away my sins. Wash me in Thy blood; fold me in Thy arms; take me to Thy heart." If you go to Him thus, He will make you His, and you shall not only be saved, but become a child of God.

It is because Christ is the Son of God, and became a child of days, that you who are children may become children of God. He became one with us when He took upon Himself our nature, and we become one with Him when we believe on Him, to the saving of our souls; and so become sons of God.

I cannot tell you how wonderful this is. John, the beloved disciple, when he thought about it, exclaimed, "Behold what manner of love the Father hath bestowed upon us, that we should be called the sons of God." And well might we wonder that such a glorious King should adopt us, and make us His children, but it is just as true as it is wonderful.

Now, to induce you to seek to be His children, I will tell you in the third place:

3. What will be your portion if you become the children of God.

(1.) If you become the children of God you will dwell forever in His presence.

The children of a king dwell near him; their home is in the palace. Your home will be in your Father's house on high. I have told you of that palace already. Would you not like such a beautiful home? You sometimes sing:

> "Beautiful Zion that I love,
> Beautiful city built above."

Do *you* love it? Would you have a mansion there? There is one provided for all who love God.

Why, some of you have friends already there. Some have a father or mother. Some brothers and sisters there. Some who have sat in these seats have entered that house with many mansions, and now dwell in the presence of God.

If I have any joy in this world it is, that under God, I directed them to seek the Saviour, and tried to comfort them with the promises of His word when God was calling them home. For it is through the dark gateway of death that we enter into the glorious city.

Before you enter into the populous part of the city of New York, there is a long dark tunnel, through which you pass, with only a little light coming down from above. All at once you come into the light of the city. Its thousand lamps, if it be night, suddenly flash their light upon you. It is a great change, coming out of the darkness into the light.

Thus it is with the city of our God. The dark passage is death. You are soon through it, and then you are into the light of that city "which has no need of sun, nor moon, nor stars, to shine in it, for God Himself doth lighten it, and the Lamb is the light thereof."

Oh what joy it would be to meet you all

there. To have you come to the end of the dark valley, just where the darkness begins to mingle with the light, to welcome me home. Or if God calls me first, what joy would it be to come out and meet you, and taking you by the hand, lead you to the Saviour, to whom I am now trying to lead you. God knows that I covet no greater reward than this. It is a sad thought to me that you do not seek the Saviour. I am so afraid that you will not become His children, and thus never dwell with Him. But again:

(2.) If you become the children of God, you will have a royal guard.

A king seldom goes far from his palace without a company of soldiers to defend him; but the children of God have a more noble guard than they.

There was once a prophet of the Lord, whose life was in jeopardy. His servant was very much frightened, but the prophet was not. He knew that God could protect him, but he did not wish his servant to be so troubled. So he prayed his eyes might be opened. God answered his prayer. And what do you think the servant saw? On the hill an exceeding great army encamped, with chariots of fire. They were the angels of the Lord of hosts, sent on purpose to defend the prophet.

Just such a guard every child of God has, for we are told that angels are ministering spirits, sent forth to minister to those who shall be the heirs of salvation. They watch over us in the darkness of night, when all are asleep; they watch over us by noon-day, so that no evil can befall us. Yes, a royal guard of angels attends all who are the children of the great King.

(3.) If you become the children of God you will have beautiful robes to wear.

Costly robes were once the mark of royal rank. "They that wear soft raiment," said Christ, "are in kings' courts." And God has provided for His children garments suitable to their high position.

You know the angel who opened up the vision to John, asked, "Who are these arrayed in white robes? and whence came they?" Their robes are those which Christ has given them—His own spotless righteousness. What garments can be more spotless than these.

We are sometimes proud of our clothing, and yet the silly sheep or the crawling worm wore them before us. It is nothing but second hand clothes that the richest and proudest wear. But the garments which Christ gives us, are *new;* fresh from His wardrobe. They will last, and retain their unsullied lustre through all eternity. And lastly:

(4.) A crown shall be yours if you become the children of God.

Did you read of the gems and jewels which adorned the young bride who was lately married to him who is to be the king of England. They were truly magnificent. If converted into money, they might have fed all the starving families in their kingdom, which are to-day crying for bread. But those jewels do not add to the happiness of any one. Under their flash and glitter there may be an aching head.

But O, the crown which Christ shall give those who are His. It is a crown of glory. It is joy to have it placed upon the brow by

His hand, and that joy shall never end. The gold may become dim, the diamond may lose its sparkle, but the crown of glory shall never fade away.

All this, children, can be yours. A home with God in heaven; a guard of angels to attend you through life; a robe of righteousness; and a crown of life.

And now let me ask you, in conclusion, Do you not desire to become the children of the great King? Can any of you refuse to come to Christ? He is standing waiting to receive you. He is saying, "Suffer the little children to come unto me." Oh, go to Him, and that too, this very day. Wait not till to-morrow, but come now. Let me lead you to the Saviour. I am going once more to commit you to Him, before we part. Pray with me when I pray; pray as soon as you go home; pray when you lie down to sleep; pray when you wake in the morning. Pray that He would make you His children, until He answers your prayers.

Seeking the Lost.

LUKE xix. 10. "The Son of Man is come to seek and to save that which was lost."

NOT many months ago two little children were lost in the woods. I do not think that you children have any idea of what a great forest is; and how impossible it is for one who is a stranger in the woods, to find his way, when once he is lost. I know that I had not, till I went away on a vacation, a year or two ago, and with some of my friends, visited that great forest, which extends along the northern part of the State of New York. After journeying two days, we secured some men who were well acquainted with that part of the country, for guides, to keep us from being lost. At first we took a bridle path, and followed it till we were under the shadow of great trees which had stood there unmolested for centuries. We could see no path, but our guide seemed to be acquainted with every tree, and knew just as well where we were as you would in the open road. We walked on and on for hours, getting deeper and deeper into the woods, till at noon-day it was almost like twilight, and we all felt that if we should lose our guides, we would never be able to get back again to our homes. At last, after a long and weary walk we came to a rude hut, where we were to pass the night. It was the only sign all around us that any body had ever been there before. The sun soon set and the darkness of night gathered around us. The light from our fire made strange shadows among the tall trees, and the gloom and darkness of the woods more profound. I shall never forget that night. Miles away from any human habitation—how still it was!—we could hear the beating of our hearts, except when the wind would moan through the branches as if it

were sighing for some sorrow which it could
not tell, or when the distant howl of the cata-
mount, or the peculiar patter of some startled
deer, crashing through the dense undergrowth,
broke the stillness.   It was a time for solemn
thoughts of our dependence upon God and of
His nearness to us, for there were the same
stars looking down upon us which were looking down upon our friends at home, and we
knew that the same God was watching over
both them and us.   To have been alone there,
or to have had no one to guide us back again,
would have made us very miserable indeed—
we should have been *lost*, we never could
have found our way home again.

But I commenced by saying that two little
children, not many months ago, were lost in
the woods.   It was just such woods as those
which I visited; nothing but trees for miles
and miles around them.   One day in spring,
they wandered away from home to gather
wild flowers, and the farther they went the
more beautiful the flowers seemed to be, till
at last it began to grow dark and they thought
of returning home.   They were sure that they

had taken the right direction. "See, see," said the little boy, for they were brother and sister, "see, see, sister, yonder's the light which mother has put in the window to guide us—no, it has gone out—yes, there it is again; don't you see it? It's gone again, but I know where it is; a tree or a bush has hid it." And on they went till their feet began to sink in the soft earth, and the little girl said, "Stop, stop, brother, that is a swamp before us "— and it was. Poor children, the light was only a will o' the wisp, which flickers over marshes, and which has many a time led astray the weary traveller. Soon they began to feel that they were lost; and oh, how sad it made them! Lost in the woods! No one near to tell them the way home! They thought of their father, their mother, of little baby brother in the cradle, and then they wept, because they might never see them any more. O, how that cry startled them. It was some wild beast prowling about at night. And they crouched down beside a tree to talk about home, and weep. And how do you think did that father and mother feel when their

children did not return, and they began to
realize that they were lost? Knowing the
danger of their children, they called together
their neighbors and friends—and very will-
ingly they helped them—to look after the lost
ones. The mother remained at home, listen-
ing every now and then at the door, for their
return, and as she listened, her lips moved in
silent prayer. What a night was that to the
poor mother—no tidings of the loved ones.
Morning dawned, and still no one came with
the joyful news that they were found. The
sun had almost finished his journey through
the heavens, and was about to set, and with
it the hope which had been cherished in the
mother's heart, when one was seen approaching the house very fast, his face beaming with
joy, to tell her that her children were found,
safe and well. Poor little things, they had
wandered farther and farther from home, and
were fainting from hunger when they were
discovered.

But I see Carrie there is thinking that this
is a very strange way of beginning a sermon,
and would like to say so to Mary if she was

not in church. But if you will read the text again you will see that the story has some-thing to do with it. "The Son of Man is come to seek and to save that which was *lost*." Lost, *lost*, that is the word in the text which I am trying to make you understand. That little boy and girl who could not find their way home were *lost*, but as we have seen, they were not so far lost but what they could be found again. But let me tell you of another way of being lost. Did you never see in the papers, "*Lost at sea.*" And did you ever try to think what it means? I will tell you by telling a story, although some of you may feel that it is but too true.

A year or two ago a boy left this village to go to sea. He was to make a long voyage. It would be months, perhaps a whole year, before he would see his home again. His friends, after a few months, received a letter from him. He was safe and well in a for-eign port, and would soon sail for home again. In due time the sailors could begin to sing, "Homeward bound," for they had weighed anchor, and were leaving the land far behind

them. Day after day passed away. Sometimes they were running before a fair wind,
and the vessel seemed almost to leap from billow to billow. Then it shifted round, and
they went this way and that way, but ever
making toward home. Sometimes the storm
raged, and the great ship was only like a
feather on the ocean; now tossed up on the
very pinnacle of some towering billow, and
then rushing down the steep sides of this
mountain of water. At last the cry was heard,
"Land! ho!" and all hearts were glad. They
would soon see their friends again. Our sail-
or boy was glad. As he took his watch at
night, he stood upon the bows, looking away
off into the darkness, in the direction of home,
and bright and pleasing were the pictures
which filled his mind. He would soon meet
his father and mother; he would soon see his
brothers and sisters; and what a happy meeting would it be, after such a long absence.
But his dreams were never to be realized; a
storm arose. Obedient to the command, he
ran up the dizzy height to execute some or-
der, his brave heart unappalled, although the

vessel was rocking from side to side, so that
the yards almost touched the water. His foot
slipped, or his hand grew tired, aud down,
down he came through the darkness, to find a
bed in the ocean. One startling cry, louder
than the blast, told of his fate—none could
rescue him. He was *lost at sea.* He sleeps
to this day in some chamber of the ocean, ·
where the storm never comes, where no mon-
ument can be placed to mark his resting place.
But ever when the storm rages, it seems to
chant the sailor boy's requiem. That is being
lost at sea. But there is still a sadder loss
than that. And now listen while I tell you
about it by telling another story.

There was once a little boy, the pride and
joy of his mother, for he had no father. He
was the only son of his mother, and she was
a widow. She had tried to bring him up to
love and serve God. When a little child, she
had taught him to pray. He was a lovely, a
noble boy. As she looked upon him, she
thought in her heart, " When I am old, my
son will comfort me ; when I walk with tottering steps, his strong arm will support me ;

and when I am upon my dying bed, he will
stand by me to wipe away the death dew from
my brow, and then close my eyes when they
can no longer discern light from darkness.
But, alas! her hopes were to be disappointed.
The time came when he had to leave home
and begin the world for himself. He had to
meet temptations, and they were too strong
for him. Evil companions became his asso-
ciates. His evenings were spent in folly and
dissipation, till at last he was what we call a
moral wreck; character, reputation all gone.
Some months ago he was sent into a gloomy
prison, to expiate by long years of unreward-
ed labor, a crime which he committed when
under the influence of the intoxicating cup.
As far as this world is concerned, he is a lost
man—lost to his mother, lost to all that is
good and noble.

But I see you are beginning to wonder why
I am telling you about children lost in the
woods; and the sailor boy lost at sea; and
still more about that boy who is to-day in the
state prison, lost forever to his mother. We
are not all lost in that sense, and I hope we

never shall be. And yet I must tell you, children, that we are all lost in a far sadder sense than any of these. Yes, hopelessly lost, had not the Son of Man come to seek and save us. And it is because of this, that I have chosen this text to-day. It is because of this, that I have just read to you about the lost sheep, and the lost piece of money, and the lost son, the prodigal who was found again. And now let me explain the text by telling you three things:

1. How we are lost.

II. Who has come to seek us.

III. How He is seeking us.

First, then, I am to tell you, how we are lost.

You sometimes sing in those beautiful hymns which you have learned:

> "Earth is a desert drear—
> *Heaven is my home.*"

But did you know, children, that unless Christ seeks after us till He finds us, there is none of us on the way to heaven. We are all (till we are found by Him) wandering, just as that little boy and girl were, away from home. Every day we are journeying farther and farther from home. It is a very sad thought, but it is true, that we are all like the prodigal son, going off into a far country, wasting our time, wasting our talents, and all that God has given us, forgetful of our Father in heaven, and of the glorious home which He has provided for us. And the strangest thing about it is that we all think, when we think about it at all, that we are going home, that *we* are not *lost*, that when we come to that dark gateway where the gloomy shadows rest, we will pass safely through to that bright home of which you sing. But this is not so; it is all a mistake. *We are all lost* till the Son of Man finds us, and begins to lead us home.

There was a little boy, who lived in the hills of Scotland, called Harry. He was much like other children—had been to church and to Sabbath school, and thought that this was all that God required of him. One day he came to church; it was the last Sabbath of the year, and the minister took for his text, 'The night is far spent, and the day is at

hand; let us put off the works of darkness,
and let us put on the armor of light." The
minister went on to show that the night—that
is, this life—was far spent, that it would soon
be over with them all, and they would then
begin an unending day with Christ in heaven,
or a long, eternal night away from Him.
Harry listened with serious attention, and the
truth went to his heart; for you know, I believe, that children not only can be, but should
be, Christians. During the night, Harry's
mother heard some one talking in his room,
and she went to see what it meant, and there
was Harry on his knees, repeating the passage,
and praying that he might put off the works
of darkness, and put on the armor of light.
He told his mother that he felt that he was
lost, and wished some one to direct him in the
way of life. Early in the morning the minister was sent for, and although it was a long
and tedious ride through the deep snow, yet
he went very cheerfully. He told Harry that
the Son of God had come to seek and save
that which was lost. And it was such good
news to him he felt it was the very Saviour

he needed, and gladly did he unite with his pastor in beseeching the good Shepherd to take him, a little lost lamb, under His care; and the prayer was heard; and that very hour he felt that he was Christ's, and come what would, he would reach home at last. It was only a few days after this, before he was safe in the good fold above. For Christ did not leave him long to wander in this world. He died, but it was a peaceful, happy death. It was only going home.

Now, children, you are all lost, just the same way that Harry was, and you all need the same Saviour. Do not think that because you are so young that it is no matter whether you are wandering away from home or not. There is nothing like *beginning* this journey right. The sooner you can say, " We're homeward bound," the better it will be for you. And now let me pass in the second place to tell you:

2. Who is seeking us.

My text says, " The Son of Man." Now this is a very strange name; a name which can only be applied to one, *the Son of Man.*

I see that Charlie, there, is ready to tell me, "I know, sir, who you mean; Christ is the Son of Man;" and that is right. But what do you think was the reason that he called Himself by that name? He sometimes, you know, called Himself the Son of God. And that is the very wonder of it, that He should be both, the *Son of God, and the Son of Man*. And let me tell you something more, that as the Son of God merely, He could never have come to seek and to save. Before He could do this, He must become the Son of Man. You know how great and glorious He was as the Son of God. He sat upon a throne of dazzling brightness, and robes of glorious majesty covered Him; there was a crown upon His brow, and a sceptre in His hand. He spake and a sun came into being, out of nothing. He spake, and worlds clustered around it. He spake, and angels and archangels, seraphim and cherubim, stood round His throne, and bowed down to worship Him, as the Creator. So glorious was He as the *Son of God*. But one day He said to the angels, "I go to seek and save the poor lost children of

c

men." And they wondered why He did not
send *them*. He told them that to do it, He
must become the *Son* of Man, and they wondered still more.

Now look and behold Him as the Son of
Man. Pause here, children, at this rude hut,
for do you not see the star, the bright star of
Bethlehem, shining over it? Let us enter in.
Why, it is a stable!—there rest the oxen in
their stalls. But see that empty manger. No,
not empty, for there sleeps a little babe there.
How beautiful He is, too. But why do those
wise men bow down to worship. There is no
glory round His brow. He looks like any
other child; and yet, children, he is the Son of
God, *as* the Son of Man. Oh! I shall never
cease wondering at this. I know I shall wonder still more if I ever get to heaven, when I
see Him in all His glory. He became a babe
that He might say, "Suffer little children to
come unto Me." He became a youth that He
might say, "Remember now thy Creator, in
the days of thy youth." He became a man
that He might say, "To you, oh men, I call,
and My voice is to the sons of men;" and that

He might lead children, youth, and those who have come to man's estate, wherever He finds them wandering, home. This is the Son of Man, and this is one of the reasons why He who was the Son of God became man. He came into the world just on purpose to seek and to save that which was lost. "But, ah," says Willie, "the Son of Man is now in heaven, for I read in the Bible about His going up from the Mount of Olives, while a cloud received Him out of sight. I wish I had lived before He went away, for then He might have found and saved me." But, Willie, He is seeking the lost now, just as much as when He was upon earth. And this leads me to tell you

3. How He is seeking us.

There was a little girl who lived in the pine woods of New Jersey, who had never heard of Christ in heaven. In this Christian land, she was a little heathen. One day a gentleman met her in the woods, and asked her the way to a certain place. She answered him very rudely. Poor little thing, she did not know any better. He got down from his horse, and sat down under the shade of a tree; and the

little shy thing kept out of his reach, for she
was afraid of him. He took from his pocket
a card, with a picture upon it, and let it float
away on the wind. The little girl soon picked it up; she had never seen any thing so beautiful before. There was one mild, sweet face
on the card, and losing her fear of the stranger, she drew near to ask him about the picture. He told her the simple story of Jesus,
and although He was in heaven now, yet He
loved children all the same as He did when
on earth. Then he taught her this little
prayer, "Lord Jesus, please make me Thy
child. Teach me how to love Thee and be
like Thee." And then he had to leave her.
Some months after, a young lady who was
sick, went to live in the woods a short time
for her health, who taught little Maggie still
more about Christ, till she felt herself to be
lost and found again. Now, Christ sought
her. He sent that good gentleman to seek
her, and then that pious lady. This is often
the way that Christ seeks after us now. He
sent me to this place for the very purpose of
seeking you. I took my Bible, for in that are

the instructions which He has given me, and there I found that I must attend to the lambs. And you know, children, how often I have invited you to come to the Saviour. I would, if I could, take you all by the hand and lead you to Him. And when I had brought you to His feet have you say, "Dear Saviour, who hast been so long seeking me, here I am, a sinful child, lost and straying; take me, lead me through this wilderness world to Thy home."

But there is another way in which Christ seeks the lost. He sends another messenger for them; be not afraid when I tell you his name—Death. He sends him and says, "Bring that little boy or girl back to Me." Since I preached to you last He has sent him twice to this place, and a short time before that, three times to one family. Into the houses he entered there was mourning and weeping, but there was rejoicing among the angels. For it was to Christ that Death took them. Death's arms were icy cold, but warm was the bosom of the Redeemer; and now He is leading little Alfred and Ellen in green pastures, and beside the still waters of His own glorious abode.

And now, children, let me ask you, Will *you* seek Christ, when He is seeking you? But *how* shall I seek Him, do you ask? By prayer. He can hear you when you call; no matter how far you may be from Him. You have only to say, " O, Thou blessed Jesus, who didst come to seek and to save the lost, I come to Thee, a poor lost wanderer. Save me for Thy mercy's sake." And He will take you in His arms, fold you to His bosom; and you shall be His forever more.

The Little Jewish Maid.

---

2 KINGS v. 2. "And the Syrians had gone out by companies, and had brought away captive, out of the land of Israel, a little maid, and she waited on Naaman's wife."

OW very quickly the weeks and months pass away, children. It seems only like a few days since I addressed you last; but nevertheless, the sixth part of a whole year has gone. We have marched along together a good way in that road which has no turnings, and no windings; which the old and the young, the grave and the gay, all travel with the same rapidity. The hours wait for no man, nor do they hasten for any. The child may wish the days that intervene between some pleasing event, gone, or the king upon his throne may wish them to linger; but heeding neither the child nor the king, the sun counts them off, neither faster nor slower than before. In his journey round this earth, the sun counts off, day after day, till at last, the great bell of heaven strikes the hour of our departure, and we are ushered into that world, where time ends, and eternity begins.

This was the first thought which i had, as I sat down to write this sermon for you. I thought that I would tell you, that you may know how fast these precious hours, with their golden opportunities, are passing. Soon I shall have preached, and you listened, to our last sermon. Bear this in mind while I speak to you, about the Little Hebrew Maid.

I must take you with me on a long journey. I do not mean that the little girl lived in a country so very far from ours, although this is true, but it is a journey back through ages —one of the journeys which never tire little feet.

We speak of travelling by steam. How

swiftly we can go, from one place to another. Twenty, thirty miles an hour, how soon it brings us to our journey's end, even if we are bound for the far West, or across the ocean. But children can travel faster than cars, or steamships. I do not mean with the body, but with the mind.

If I should say to you, *imagine* yourselves among the heathery hills of Scotland, or in the crowded streets of London—without the least effort, you could think of yourselves as there. It is such a journey that I wish you to take with me to-day, and I will see that it is a Sabbath day's journey, for it will be to the land of the Bible.

Come with me, then, and let us stand, not beside the city of David, but at the well of Jacob; the same well at which the Lord of life begged water from a woman of Samaria, and gave to her the living water.

What a beautiful country! How tall and graceful are these trees which adorn Mount Gerizim. A holy man lives here—the prophet of Israel. See him, with his long white beard, and flowing locks. How mild and

c5

pleasant he looks, just the man to multiply
the widow's oil—just the man to restore to life
the son of the weeping Shunamite.

Look well at the house into which he is entering. What a house! do you say, for a prophet? It is true, it is nothing better than a
mean hut. But let me tell you, children, and
I wish you to remember it—the greatest men
do not live in palaces. To this day, you will
find more truly good and great men, in peas-
ants' huts, than in lordly halls.

But, stand back, stand back. Do you not
see that cloud of dust yonder? Do you not
hear the rumbling of chariot wheels, and the
trumpet's loud blast? It is some great man
passing through the land, in state, and he
needs to tell how great he is in this manner.
He must be going to the king's palace. No,
he has just left the royal mansion, and see, he
stops at the prophet's humble door.

One of his servants knocks, imperiously,
and tells them within, that Naaman, the Syrian, the great and successful general, has
come to see the prophet, that he may cleanse
him of his leprosy. For, although, a great

man, he has that most loathsome and incurable disease. And yet, so proud of heart is he, that instead of humbly asking, he almost demands this favor from the prophet.

But, see how the man of God treats him. You might think that the poor prophet would come out with all haste to do him homage, considering himself highly honored by a visit from such an illustrious personage. But he did no such thing. Naaman was only the servant of the king of Syria; but Elisha was the servant of the most High God.

Men may talk about titles, and noble birth, and an illustrious ancestry, but I tell you, children, that the highest title a man can have in this world, the most honorable position which he can occupy, is to be, and to be called, a servant of Christ. Whenever you hear any one speaking of *noble men*, just ask them if they are Christian men, for *the good alone are great.* But I must not forget the story.

Elisha did not go out to meet Naaman. He merely sent him a message by his servant Gehazi: "Go wash seven times in Jordan."

c6

Oh, how angry proud Naaman was. Why, said he, " I thought he would come out to my chariot, and call upon the name of his God, and strike his hand over the place, and recover me of the leprosy. But, instead of this, to tell me to go and wash in Jordan, that mean little river! Why not in some of the noble rivers of Damascus ?"

Fine talk this, for a poor but proud leper. His servants know better, and persuaded him to renounce his pride, and do as he was commanded. And as the prophet told, he is cured of his fearful disease.

But now you may ask, how did Naaman know about the prophet in Israel, and that he could recover him of his leprosy ?

You know the Syrians did not like the children of Israel, and the children of Israel did not like them. They were idolaters. They worshipped the god Rimmon, who was no God. They did not believe in the God of Abraham, whom the Jews worshipped, and who is the only true God.

Well, I will tell you how Naaman came to know about Elisha. Some time before, the

Syrians had gone out by companies, for the purpose of plundering the Israelites. They were cruel, hard-hearted men. Not only did they take herds and flocks for spoil, but also little children, as captives, and kept or sold them as slaves. Among these was a little maid, and she was given as a present to Naaman's wife, and she waited on her.

I think I see that little girl, when her services are not needed, going out to weep in some quiet place. Perhaps her father and mother were both killed by Naaman's cruel men of war. She sighs for her own native land. She thinks of the green trees, and shady groves : of the beautiful temple, and the long line of white-robed priests, who offer the sacrifices at the altar. She will not go · into the temple of Rimmon—they cannot make her bow down to an idol. But morning, noon, and night, she prays to the God of her fathers, and asks Him to be her God, although she may never tread the courts of the temple again. And having prayed well, she lives well.

She forgets the cruelty of Naaman—she

forgets the wrong which he has done her.
She knows how to forgive an injury—she
pities him, as she sees him a poor leper, and
very modestly says to her mistress, " Would
God, my lord were with the prophet that is
in Samaria, for he would recover him of his
leprosy." How did she know that he could,
or would, for Elisha had never healed any
one before. She knew that the man of God
had great power, and had performed many
wonderful miracles. She had faith to believe,
that if he could do these things, the God who
had given him this power would also enable
him to heal the captain of the Syrian host.
She never thinks for a moment, that he might
refuse to do it, and that Naaman might come
home in anger, and destroy her for sending
him on such a useless errand. She has stronger faith than this. How many prayers did
she offer for her master, as he went on his
journey. How acceptable were they to the
prayer-hearing God. What a reward, too,
was hers, for she was the means, under
God, of the conversion of this poor heathen. To-day, in heaven, that little He-

brew maid has a big bright jewel in her crown of glory.

We are not told what Naaman did when he returned home. We know this much, that he could not be a hard and cruel master, since he was a converted man.

This, then, is the story of the little Hebrew maid. I have told you a *long story*, but I mean to preach a *short sermon* about it. This story teaches us three things:

I. *Children* can be Christians.

II. Christian children can do much good.

III. Such children will have a glorious reward.

First, then, I am to show you from this story, that:

I. Children can be Christians.

Now, I see plainly that some of you are thinking, why, this was not a Christian child. She was a Jewess, and the Jews did not love Christ. They were the wicked men who crucified Him.

Ah, but children, do you not know that there were a great many pious Jews, who

worshipped God, and longed and prayed for
the time when Christ would come.

But how could she be a Christian before
Christ came into the world? I will tell you :
she believed in a Saviour to come, just as we
believe in a Saviour who has already come.

But, says Mary, I did not know that religion was any thing that children should trouble themselves about. Why, I thought it
was only for old people, or for those who were
just going to die. Then they send for the
minister, and have him pray that God would
forgive them their sins, for Jesus' sake, and
take them to heaven, if they should not get
well.

A great many think just like you, Mary.
But I cannot begin to tell you how wrong it is.
I have wondered time and again, how any
can feel thus. I try to tell them differently,
but it is only now and then, that one seems to
believe; not what I say—that would be nothing, but what God has said in his word. He
says, "They that seek Me early shall find
Me." He represents Himself as being near to
children, and says, "Seek ye the Lord, while

He is near, call ye upon Him while He may be found." And yet they say by their actions, "We will not be in a hurry—we will wait."

Let me tell you a story, a true story, and this will show you how dangerous it is to wait.

A friend of mine told me story about a lad who attended his church during a revival of religion. He seemed to be very attentive, but he was not a Christian. When asked if he did not desire to become a Christian, he answered, "Oh, there is time enough yet, I am young, and a few years will make no difference." Three short weeks passed away. The minister was called to see that boy on a sick, and as it proved to be, a dying bed. He asked him again, "Is it not time to seek the Saviour *now?*" "Oh, sir," said the dying boy, "it is *too late, too late.* My time was when you spoke to me before," and the last words he uttered were, "*too late, too late.*"

But I know that children think they cannot be Christians. We do not know how old this little Hebrew maid was; but as we have seen, she was a Christian. And ι can tell you about a great many children, who loved and served the Saviour in the days of their youth. Here is one:

Anna G—— was only nine years of age. Many a time did she think thus in her heart: I wish I was a Christian. Could she be a Christian so young? Yes, younger children than she have been Christians, and why not Anna? She had pious parents. When she was only a little babe they had given her to God, and prayed for her every day that He would make her His child. She had been taught a great deal about God and heaven, and all good things. But still she said, I am not a Christian, and I don't know how to be one. After thinking a great deal about it, and praying a great many times to the Lord to teach her, and shedding a great many tears over her naughtiness, she one day made this resolution:

I don't know as I shall ever be a Christian, and feel that Jesus has pardoned all my sins, but this I will do. I will give myself to the Saviour every day of my whole life. I will read my Bible, and pray that my sins may be forgiven, and then *I will try and act just as Christians do.* So Anna commenced to do as she had said, and the blessed Saviour listened to her prayers, forgave her sins, and accepted her as His child. She was a Christian.

And now, children, why not follow Anna's example? Why wait, when the Saviour has sent me to invite you to come to Him. I wish I could make you all leave the house of God this day with the same resolution. Why, there would be rejoicing not only among the thousands of little children in heaven, but also among the angels of God.

But I must pass to the second part of this sermon:

2. Children can not only become Christians, but they can also do a great deal of good in the world.

Had God said to an angel in heaven, " Whether would you rather be, the king of Syria, with all his gold and silver and armies, or that little Hebrew maid, who is a captive, but loves and serves Me, and who has been the

means of sending Naaman, the leper, to My
prophet in Samaria?" the angel would not
have paused a moment, before he answered:
" The little Hebrew maid. She has done something which will always be remembered."

It is just thus that God and angels look at
this life. God gives us all opportunities of
doing good. And He wishes us to improve
them. The great trouble with us all is that
we do so little for Christ, even when we begin
to serve Him in our youth. Why, when we
think of what we have done for Christ, it
makes us blush for shame.

But I see Lizzie there, would like to say,
" But, sir, although children may become Christians, you surely mean that they must be old
enough to join the Church, and be Sabbath
school teachers, before they can serve Christ."

No, I mean just what I said, that *children*
can serve Him. Why, it is serving Christ to
go to the sick bed of a dying child, and hold
to its parched lips a cup of cold water, in His
name. It is serving Christ, if we are first
Christians ourselves, to pray that He would
convert our brothers, sisters, and playmates.

It is serving Christ, to tell about Jesus, and invite others to come to Him. It is serving Christ, to give our little mite to send a tract or a Testament to some heathen child, if we pray for God's blessing to accompany it.

Here I must tell you another story, to show you how a little girl served Christ.

There was a little German girl, I cannot tell you her name, for I do not know it, who had for the first time in her life, entered a Protestant church. She there heard of Christ as a Saviour, and before she left the church she had found Him. So easy is it to find Christ when we seek Him with our whole heart.

Full of joy and wonder, she ran home to tell her father, who was a bigoted Roman Catholic, what a Saviour she had found. But to her surprise, he became very angry, and beat her cruelly, and forbade her to mention the subject again in his house.

She, however, continued to attend the church, and expressed a desire to become a member, that she might partake of the bread and wine—the memorials of Christ's broken

body and shed blood. Her father told her if
she did, he would beat her to death.

But you know, children, Christ has said,
" If any one love father or mother more than
Me, he is not worthy of Me." She loved
Christ best, and obeyed His command. When
she returned home and told her father what
she had done, he beat her unmercifully and
drove her from the house, telling her never to
return again until she had given up the new
religion.   There is a promise in the Word of
God, " When thy father and mother forsake
thee, the Lord will take thee up."   God
never forgets His promises, and as we might
expect, He provided for this little girl.   And
now I will tell you how she tried to serve
Christ.

The first Monday in every month she spent
in distributing tracts to all the German families of her acquaintance ; never passing by
her father's house, although sure of being
beaten and driven from it.   But she said, " I
did not care for the blows, for my father's
poor soul was all I thought of."

How long do you think she kept this up ?

A month? two months? Yes, for eighteen months; praying all the time that God would convert her poor father.

After having visited him so long, with the same treatment every time, he suffered her to read, converse, and pray with him. The next month, with tears in his eyes, he begged his daughter to forgive him, and pray for him. And he knelt down and prayed, too, although all he could say was, " O, Lord, forgive; O, Lord, forgive." And before long she had the satisfaction of knowing that her father had also found the Saviour.

Can children do nothing for Christ? How many grown-up Christians will such an example put to the blush! Did the children but begin to serve Christ, how much good could they do.

But I have only a little more to say about the last head of this sermon, and I am done.

3. The reward which such children will receive.

There is a beautiful verse in the very last book of the Bible, which are the words of Christ Himself. I never read it but what it

seems as though Christ was speaking to me
from heaven. It is this: "Behold I come
quickly, and My reward is with Me, to give
every man according as his works shall be."
It seems as if Christ was saying, Work dili-
gently, for I will soon come for thee; and as
you labor, think of the glorious reward. What
is this reward? A crown of life which fadeth
not away, and somehow or other I think there
will be a star in that crown for every soul
that we have led to Christ. Some will have
crowns without a single star; some will have
one or two; while others will have a diadem
of stars.

The little Hebrew maid will have one bright
star at least, and so will that little German
girl; Paul and Peter will have so many that
we will not be able to number them. How
will it be with you, my child? Do you not
desire to work for Christ? Come, then, to
Him, and having given yourself to Him, work
with all your might. Speak to your companions about the blessed Saviour. Send Bibles
and tracts to the heathen, and Sabbath school
missionaries and libraries to the poor children

in the far West. God will watch over your little offerings. He knows the book your money bought. He knows all the good it has done. And when you stand before His judgment seat, some will rise up and call you blessed. You never saw them; they are strangers to you. But Christ will make them known. That heathen child heard of Christ from the little book your money purchased. That child from your own land was brought to the Saviour by the little tract you sent. And Christ will say, These are the fruits of your labors; and placing a crown upon your brow, He will say, This is your reward.

God grant that you may all have starry crowns in *that day*.

The Snow Sermon.

PSALM li. 7. "Wash me, and I shall be whiter than snow."

WHAT a beautiful world this is, children; beautiful in winter as well as in summer; beautiful in fall as well as in spring. I know that each has a different kind of beauty, and it is all the better for this, because we love variety. Were it all sunshine, day after day, we should get tired of it. Were the fields always green, the flowers ever blooming, we should forget all about their beauty and long for some change. So you see God has wisely ordered it that the grand panorama should be different. No two days are just alike. It is as if He was changing the great picture which He has spread out before us, every day; permitting us to see it to-day in one light, to-morrow in another. Now dipping His pencil in deepest green, now in gold and crimson, and then again spreading a covering of snow over all, as pure and spotless as if He had dropped down upon earth the curtain which conceals His glorious throne.

Did you notice yesterday, children, how silently the snow fell from heaven. Flake after flake came down here and there, as if they were things of life, as if each one of them wished to fall just in its own place. When you looked across the fields it was one unbroken plain of white; many of the deformities of earth were concealed. It reminded me of the mantle of charity, which hides a multitude of sins.

There is something grand in a snow storm, especially if you look out upon it from your own comfortable homes, and know that there is no one suffering around you; that even the poorest child in our midst is sheltered from the cold, and can warm itself beside the cheer-

ful fire. I know that children love the snow.
Their eyes sparkle with delight as they watch
the first flakes flying through the air, and
their busy imaginations revel in the prospect
which is before them. We love to have them
feel so. We would not, if we could, dispel
their happy dreams. We would rather join
them in their sports, and help them to enjoy
their innocent amusements.

But I am afraid that you are beginning to
think about your play, which, you know,
would not be right in the house of God.
This is the day in which we should forget, as
much as possible, all about this world, and
think about that other world, to which we are
all going. I know, too, that some of you are
wondering what I have to tell you about the
snow. Were this the time and place, I think
I could tell you a great many curious things
about it. I would advise you the next snow
storm to go out, and take a sheet of paper
with you; catch upon it a few of the largest
flakes; be careful not to break them; look at
them before they melt, and you will be sur-
prised to find how beautiful they are. As

beautiful and delicate as tne leaves of the fairest flowers ; so that you will almost think that they are the spotless blossoms of a fairer world showered down upon this earth in richest profusion.

But it is about time that I had given you the name of this sermon. It is to be the Snow Sermon. I know you will all remember this.

There are only a very few places in the Bible where there is any thing said about snow. I wish you would all look them out. The reason why so little is said about it in the Bible is, because it was written in a country where they had but very little snow. It was only once in a while that they saw the fields in this pure dress. Christ did not speak about it once, but His disciples did. When He was transfigured, Peter, James, and John, who then saw His glory, said His raiment was white as *snow*. And then again, when John saw Him in heaven, a great many years after Christ had left this world, he said that His head and His hair were white as snow. Had the Bible been written in a land like this, I have no doubt Christ would have had much to say about it. For He always took the most familiar things in nature to illustrate His instructions, so that they might always remind His hearers of the gracious words which He spake. And it is because I like to follow the example of Christ, the great Teacher, that I have taken the words of David for my text. Let us read them again. *Wash me and I shall be whiter than snow.* You see, children, that it is a prayer offered by him who was called the man after God's own heart. And it is just the prayer that we all need to offer, both old and young. For unless we have it answered by Him who heareth prayer, we can never dwell in His holy, happy home.

Now I will tell you:

I. What is meant by this prayer.

II. Why we all need to offer it.

III. The encouragement which we have that God will answer it.

First, then, what is meant by this prayer.

The youngest of you know that there is nothing in this world whiter than snow. When we say, as white as snow, we mean just as white as can be made, without the least speck or blemish. But I can explain this best by telling you a story—a Bible story.

The night on which our Lord was betrayed into the hands of His enemies, to be crucified, He was with His disciples in an upper room. And as they sat talking in low and mournful strains (for Christ, their Master, felt very sad, and they sympathized with Him), He rose up and took a towel, and girded Himself with it, and a basin with water, and began to wash the feet of His disciples. When He came to Peter he was astonished that the other disciples should let their great and glorious Master take the place of a servant for them, and said, "No, Lord, Thou shalt never wash my feet." Jesus knew what he meant, for you know He could read the heart, and said to him, "Peter, if I wash thee not, thou hast no part in Me;" that is, you cannot be My disciple. Then said Peter, "Not my feet only, but my hands and my head."

I need not tell you that neither Christ, nor David, nor Peter, meant by this washing the cleansing of the body. That is comparatively a small matter.   But there is something which is all important, that is, *the cleansing of our hearts.*

Job asked, a great many years ago, "Who can bring a clean thing out of an unclean?" that is, who can make a sinful heart holy? And he had to answer, "Not one." No man can do this.   Sin is a stain which we cannot remove from our souls.   We may weep bitter tears of sorrow, but these will not take it away.   We may, like the monks of old, make pilgrimages, scourge ourselves, fast till we become emaciated like skeletons, but the black stain is still upon our hearts.   And it would be sad indeed if we had to tell you that no one could make a sinful soul holy, or a guilty heart clean.   There is One, and only One, who can do this, and that is God.   I will tell you pretty soon by what means He does this. But first I will tell you a story, by which I hope to make what I have been saying, more plain.

There was a little boy, we will call him Eddie, for I have forgotten his name, it is so long since I heard the story.   He was upon the whole, a pretty good boy, but he had some faults, and wished to overcome them. His father proposed a plan. He told Eddie that every time he committed one of these faults he might drive a nail into a post, and every time he was tempted to commit the fault, but *resisted*, he might pull out one of the nails. It was a very successful plan. After a year of hard struggles, there stood the post without a single nail in it. "Well done, my son," said his father to him; "you have been a brave boy, to conquer these bosom enemies. There is not a single nail in the post now." But the little boy was sad. "What is the matter," said his father, kindly. "O," said the son, "the *nails* are all gone, but the *marks* are left." That is true; even when we conquer our faults, the marks remain upon our hearts. And this should trouble us. For, just think how we would appear in heaven, beside the holy angels, should God take us there, without removing the stains from our souls.

There was once a man who had committed a great crime, for which he was condemned to die. The day for his execution drew near. The then President of the United States was told one day that a lady wished to see him on very important business. An interview was granted. To his surprise, a lady and six children knelt at his feet, imploring for the life of the husband and father. The President stood for some time in amazement, and then the big tears began to chase each other down his cheeks, and his voice was choked so that he could not speak. With his eyes streaming with tears, and his hands raised toward heaven, he pushed a way out of the room, and in a few moments returned with a paper in his hand. It was a free pardon for her husband. He was pardoned, and that very day released from prison, but he was still conscious of his sin. It troubled him by night and by day. He felt as though every body was pointing at him and saying, "There is a man who deserved to die, but was pardoned through the intercession of his wife and the kindness of the President."

Now this would be the case with us did God from heaven, "I will pardon you all," but had provided no way to remove the stains of sin from our souls. We could not be happy. We should feel as though angels were saying, " What sin-defiled creatures these are. Look at the black stains upon their souls." And, children, if this was the way that God saved us, heaven would be no heaven to us. We could not be happy in such a holy place.

But now I will tell you what God does for us, and then you will see what the prayer of the text means. You know that there are some things which will take out even the blackest stains. But what think you could take away the stains from our hearts? Only one thing in the whole universe—*the blood of Christ*. This must be applied to our hearts, and then, although they are all defiled with sin, they become white as snow. Not only are the nails taken out, but the *marks* of the nails are removed.

But, do you ask how David knew any thing about the blood of Christ? For you all know that David lived a great many years before Christ died upon the cross. I will tell you. You must come with me to the tabernacle for the temple was not yet built, and you will see how David learned it.

The people have been looking for a long time for a red heifer; red from horn to hoof, without a single white spot upon it. It was to be a type of Him who was red in His apparel, and His garments like one that treadeth in the wine press. They have found it, and there it stands, meek and patient. Let us see what they will do with it. They lead it without the camp. You know they crucified Christ outside of the walls of the city, and this was a prophecy of Him in type. There it is struck down with a blow, and as its life's blood flows away, they catch it in a dish, and take it to the high-priest. The body they cast upon the altar, till it is consumed to ashes. These ashes are gathered by the hand of a fit man, and are kept in a sacred place, as a precious treasure. When a man has sinned, the high-priest takes some of these ashes and puts them in water, and with a bunch of hyssop sprinkles them upon the defiled man, and he is pronounced clean.

It was in this manner that David and the

rest of the Jews were taught to look away down to distant ages, when God's own sacrifice should come, who could take away sin. Hence he prayed, " Purge me with hyssop and I shall be clean ; wash me and I shall be whiter than snow." He wished that precious blood, which was even then just as if it had been shed, applied to his heart. And God answered his prayer.

Now, children, this is all very wonderful, but it is just as true as it is wonderful. There are this day multitudes in heaven who were sinners once, like you and me, but they are now before the throne, pure as snow ; pure as the angels, who never sinned in thought, in word, or in deed. They have washed their robes and made them white in the blood of the Lamb.

But some of you may say, " Perhaps it is only little stains which this blood can take away. Great sins, sins which are black as darkness, cannot be removed." It is not so. One of the most comforting texts in the whole Bible for poor sinful creatures such as we are, is where God tells us this very thing. He

D

says, and He is speaking to you and to me, "Come now, and let us reason together, saith the Lord: though your sins be as scarlet, they shall be as white as snow; though they be red like crimson, they shall be as wool." And then, in another place, "The blood of Christ cleanseth from all sin."

This, then, is what is meant by the prayer for God to take away the stains of guilt from our souls. But I must haste now to tell you in the second place:

2. Why each of us should offer this prayer.

The first reason is, because we are all sinners. It is a very solemn truth, children, that the very youngest of you have sinned against God. We know that some speak about *innocent childhood*, but where does wicked manhood come from? Did I ever tell you about the painter who wished to make two great pictures; one to represent Innocence, the other to represent Guilt? He saw at last a beautiful baby boy, sleeping in his mother's arms. He had dimpled, rosy cheeks, and a smile so pure upon his face, that it seemed as though the angels must be whispering to him in his slumber. He painted the likeness of this child, and every one said, "How sweet; how innocent."

Years passed away. The artist had not yet found his ideal of guilt. He saw many hardened wretches, but there was always some redeeming feature in their countenances. At length he visited a prison, and saw there a man bloated and besotted by sin. Every vice seemed to be written on his face. He took his portrait, and hung it up beside the other. What a contrast! Every one smiled as they looked at the one, and shuddered as they looked at the other, and said, Is it possible that any one could be so wicked as that? But what was the artist's surprise when he found that it was one and the same person he had painted. The beautiful babe had become the wicked man.

Now, what I wish to show you, is this. In these little hearts of yours there are the seeds of sin; small now, but if you let them alone they will soon become so great that you cannot root them out.

You have all seen an acorn. The smallest

child can take it in his hand. It is no bigger than a marble. But put it in the ground and in a few years it will become a great tree, so that the birds can build in its branches. I once saw a young lion. It was as harmless as a lamb. You could play with it without the least danger. In the next cage there was a full-grown lion. There was murder in his eye. When he shook his shaggy mane and opened his strong jaws crying for blood, the other beasts trembled. I knew that in a few years the young lion would be just like him.

It is just so with these hearts of ours. Before the seeds of evil take root and grow, we know not how wicked we can become. Left to ourselves, children, we might become the vilest of sinners. It is only the grace of God that keeps us from this. You may say, I will never do so and so; I will never commit such a sin as that. But you do not know. You cannot tell. You are not safe unless you have prayed to God, "Wash me and I shall be whiter than snow." For you are all sinners, and have need of this cleansing. This is the second reason why we should all offer this prayer.

Because *God* only, can take away our sins. I cannot take away my own sins, much less yours. I can only tell you how you may be cleansed from all iniquity. By praying to God that He would wash you in the blood of Christ. The precious blood of His Son, applied to your hearts, will make them fair and beautiful. O, that I could persuade you to offer this prayer with all your hearts.

But says Mary, "How do you know, sir, that God would do this great thing for me, if I should ask Him?" Let me ask you, Mary, Do you feel that it would be a *great thing* to be cleansed by the blood of Christ? Do you desire this above every thing else? If you do, then I can answer your question, and this will be the third and last thing that I have to say about the text.

III. The encouragement which we have to offer this prayer.

We have the promise of God Himself. What, do you say, "has God promised to do this for me?" *Yes, for you.* Do you say,

"O, sir, where is that promise to be found?
I have never seen it." Then I will repeat it
for you. Listen, for it is very important:
"Thus saith the Lord, I will be inquired of
by the house of Israel, to do this thing for
them." That means nothing more nor less,
than I will do this for every one that asks me,
"Then will I sprinkle clean water upon you,
and ye shall be clean."

Now you know that God always fulfills His
promises. I never yet found a man who could
say God made a promise but did not keep it.
Far from it. I have found many who could
say His promises are many and great, but He
has more than fulfilled them all.

Now, children, will you not go to Him? It
is a simple prayer. You have to ask Him
earnestly: "Wash me, O Lord, that I may
be made whiter than the snow, for Jesus'
sake;" and He will hear and answer this
prayer.

I wonder if I have made this plain, so that
you can all understand it. I have tried to
impress upon you one of the lessons which the
snow teaches. When you see it falling in

pure white flakes, not only think of this prayer, but offer it. When you see the earth covered with its white robes, think of those who stand before the throne of God in raiment pure and white. And then ask, Am I preparing to be one of their number ?

Let me assure you, children, that if you and I, with our whole hearts, present this petition to God, day by day, in a little while we shall meet in yonder bright world, and there sing together the song of salvation ; saying, " Unto Him who loved us, and gave Himself for us, and has washed us in His blood, and made us kings and priests to our God, be honor and glory, dominion and might forever. Amen."

D4

The Little Fox Hunters.

Song ii. 15. "Take us the foxes, the little foxes that spoil the vines; for our vines have tender grapes."

I AM sure that I have a text to-day, which some of you have never heard before. I think you would almost say that it is not in the Bible. Did you notice that I did not tell you, as I usually do, where the text is to be found. I wished to see if any one of you could tell. Let me repeat it again: "Take us the foxes, the little foxes that spoil the vines; for our vines have tender grapes." Now, do any of you know in what book of the Bible that is to be found? You don't know? Well, I will tell you, for you might look a long time before you found it:

Song of Solomon, the 2d chapter and 15th verse, is the place. And as you have already supposed, this is to be a fox sermon, " *The little foxes, and how to catch them.*"

I see Tommy and Charlie there, looking at each other as if they thought this must be a very interesting sermon, and I hope that I shall be able to set them and all the rest of you fox hunting, without even waiting till after the Sabbath.

Let me remind you first of all, that Christ spoke about foxes several times. One day when He was preaching out in the fields—I think it must have been about sunset—and as He looked abroad He saw the birds flying to their nests, and perhaps a fox slyly peeping forth from its burrow, for you know they live under ground. He pointed to these, saying to the great multitude who had come to hear Him preach, "See how the birds of the air are flying to their nests as the evening shadows begin to lengthen. See how the cunning fox is peeping forth from his hole where he finds a secure shelter. But here am I, who taught the little birds to build their nests and

5A

the fox to provide for itself a home; and yet
because I am now the Son of Man, I have not
where to lay my weary head. In this world
—although I made it all—I have no home of
my own; I must beg this very night a lodg-
ing from some of you." Well, that is one of
the passages in which Christ speaks about
foxes. But let me tell you something which
may sound very strange to some of you, and
that is, our text is another place where Christ
is speaking, too. It is He who is saying,
" Take us the foxes, the little foxes that spoil
the vines; for our vines have tender grapes."

I know that I have told you that the text
was in the Song of Solomon. But it was
Christ who told Solomon to write this beautiful song. It is the only dialogue in the Bible. Sometimes it is Christ who is speaking,
and sometimes it is His church, but never
Solomon, as Solomon. It is Solomon as a
Christian, and every Christian should be able
to speak of Christ and to Christ just as the
king of Israel did, and should be able to hear
Christ speaking to him every time he reads
this beautiful language.

The Christian, in verse 10th, tells us what Christ said to him: "My beloved," that is Christ, "said unto me, Rise up my love, my fair one, and come away; for lo! the winter is past, the rain is over and gone, the flowers appear on the earth, the time of the singing of birds is come, and the voice of the turtle is heard in our land." That is the spring-time of the soul when a man or a child becomes a Christian; it is just like the passing away of a long and dreary winter. There is bright sunlight in the soul. In the cold and barren heart flowers begin to spring up; such flowers as angels love to look upon; flowers which will never wither, but bloom and expand in the bright sunlight of heaven.

Then Christ speaks again in the 14th verse: "O my dove," that is the affectionate name He calls you and me if we are His. "O my dove, that art in the clifts of the rock"—a timid bird, hiding away from danger—"let me see thy countenance, let me hear thy voice; for sweet is thy voice, and thy countenance is comely. Take us the foxes, the little foxes

that spoil the vines; for our vines have ten
der grapes."

You see, then, that Christ speaks to us just
as much in the Song of Solomon, as in the
Gospels. These are gracious words. But
what do they mean? That is just what I am
going to tell you, for this is one reason why I
preach to the children, to teach them to understand the "Word of God." I will therefore tell you what is meant by the little foxes
that spoil the vines, and how to catch them.

First, then, I am to tell you

I. What is meant by the little foxes.

I never saw a fox but once. He was a sly,
roguish-looking fellow. He did not look right
ahead, as all honest animals, and honest men,
too, do, but out of the corner of his eye, as if
he would make you believe that he was quite
innocent, when all the time he was looking
for an opportunity to do some mischief.

In the land where the Bible was written
there were a great many foxes, and they did
much harm. Fences were made around the
vineyards to keep out the cattle of the fields
and the wild beasts of the woods, and they

answered a good purpose. But through the smallest holes, the foxes, especially the *little foxes*, would creep at night, and spoil the vines and destroy the tender grapes; for they are very fond of grapes. In those vineyards they had a tower in the centre, where a man was placed to watch. If a robber came, or a wild beast managed to break through, the noise they made would alarm the watchman, and he could drive them off or call for help. Think of him watching through the long night, never closing his eyes for a moment, and supposing that all was right, going forth in the morning and finding here and there fine clusters of grapes upon the ground, or even some of the best young vines destroyed. Would it not be provoking? He would say, "Those foxes, those little foxes, I must make some traps to catch them or they will destroy all the young vines."

But you say, there are neither foxes nor vineyards here; what good is there in telling us how to catch the foxes? Let me tell you, children, that each one of *you* has a very fine and valuable vineyard, that it has many precious vines, which should bring forth rich clusters of grapes, but the foxes, the little foxes, spoil some of the very best of them. I will now try and make this plain, for it is no use to preach to the children unless they can understand you. This vineyard is your heart. Do you say, How strange to call my heart a vineyard? It may seem strange to you, but let me explain it.

You know a vineyard is a place where you expect to find fruit. So God expects to find fruit in our hearts. What kind of fruit? He made your hearts to love and serve Him, and He expects to find this beautiful flower growing there. At first only a small blossom, so that you can say, I hope I love Him; I wish I did love Him; I think I do love Him. And then this blossom should grow till it becomes fruit, so that you can say, I *do* love God, but O I long to love Him more. And then the little bud will expand, and expand, till in its ripeness and beauty He transplants both vine and vineyard to heaven.

I say, this is what God expects, but it is not what He always finds. He looks into our hearts, but alas! children, He often finds nothing but weeds there—neither blossoms nor fruit. It is like a long-neglected garden, all run to weeds. This should not be so, for Christ has done a great deal for us, so that our hearts might bring forth good fruit to His honor and glory.

You know that once we all belonged to Satan rather than to Christ. And Satan is not merely a fox, but a great roaring lion, going about seeking whom he may devour. There is nothing which troubles Satan more than to see any good in our hearts. He would trample all the vines under his feet, and rejoices very much when he has sown our hearts full of tares, so that no good seed can have a chance to grow.

The first thing Christ had to do for us, was to bring us back from the power and dominion of Satan. Do you know the price He had to pay? Nothing less than His own most precious blood. And now He comes to us with His mild and winning voice and says, "I have bought you with My blood that you may become a part of My vineyard. Will you be Mine? I will root out all the foul weeds which are in your hearts, and plant in their stead choice vines, which shall bear good fruit."

I told you in my last sermon all about this cleansing—how Christ can make your black hearts as white as snow; and now I will tell you how Christ can make your hearts, after they are cleansed with His blood, fruitful vineyards.

The other day, as I was returning from visiting one of the Sabbath school children, who is sick, I saw a man working in an orchard. It looked to me as if he was spoiling one of the trees. He had cut off some of the finest branches. I thought that would never do; so I stepped in and asked him what he was about. "O," says he, "I'm grafting. These limbs which I have cut off would never bear good fruit, so I am taking them away and putting slips from good trees in their place." He had in his hand a few small shoots, and after cutting into the tree, he placed them in the slits he had made, and then fastened them securely in their places. He told me that this tree, which was bad by nature, would in a few years bring forth good fruit.

This is just the way that Christ manages with us. He is the true vine. And He grafts our hearts with slips from Himself, so that we bear the same kind of fruit that Christ did when He was upon earth. I have told you of love to God, and love to Christ, which is the same thing. This is the first fruit which grows in our hearts after we have submitted to Him. Then comes love to our fellow men. You know, children, that this is a very selfish world. We are all apt to love ourselves far more than we ought, and not love others as much as we should. But when we become Christ's, we love Him more and more, and then love every body for Jesus' sake.

Let me here tell you of a little boy who did not seem to care for any body but himself. He was very bright and intelligent. He went to the best schools, and became in time a very learned man. His friends were all proud of him. His father, as he listened to one of his speeches in the synagogue, for he was a Jewish boy, could hardly refrain from saying, That is my son Saul, who has come back from Jerusalem to Tarsus. They call him now Rabbi Saul; that is, Saul the Teacher. But all his learning did him no good. At that time he hated Christians, and asked for letters that he might cast into prison all who called upon the name of Christ. But Christ obtained possession of his heart. And you would no longer recognize in the disciple of Jesus, Saul the persecutor. The little shoot which Christ planted in his heart brought forth much fruit.

He knew that there were a great many who had never heard of Jesus; so he went to tell them of the Saviour he had found. They sometimes stoned him, sometimes cast him into prison, sometimes beat him with rods, but he loved them so that he still kept on, telling them about Christ, and entreating them to come to Him and be saved. All this was only the fruit from the vine which Christ had planted in his heart. And, children, you may become the same if you will only give your hearts to Christ.

But dear me, I do not wonder that some of you should be ready to ask, What, sir, have you done with the foxes? Now, I must tell you about them, and you will understand it all the better if I give their names.

There are a great many very little foxes which no bars nor bolts, no hedge nor fence can keep out of your hearts. They are called *wicked thoughts*, and they do spoil the tender grapes. They sometimes come one at a time, and sometimes they come in great numbers, as it were, chasing each other through the vineyard. But in whatever manner they come they do a great deal of mischief. You all know what I mean. It is impossible to be good when our hearts are filled with wicked thoughts.

I will tell you about one of these little foxes that came into my vineyard the other day, and came very near destroying a whole bunch of grapes. It was just after I had been preaching to the children the last time. This little fox said to me, "It is no use preaching to the children. You do not interest them. They do not listen. You had better give it

up." And I was very foolish, for I let him
run about for almost a week without setting
a trap to catch him. Well, one day I heard
of a little boy, who is not here to-day—he is at
home very sick—who said, that he had been
very much interested in that very sermon, and
that he was trying to be a better boy. So I
said this little fox will trouble me no more.
I will catch him and kill him. And I think
I have finished him.

But another of the little foxes which spoil
the grapes is called Pride. He is a cunning
little fellow. He nestles in the heart, in some
warm corner and makes us do all manner of
naughty things. He makes us think that we
are better than other people, and sometimes
causes us to say wicked things, which hurts
their feelings.

Then there is Mr. Deceit. Many a good
bunch of grapes he has spoiled. That is the
little fox which makes us pretend, when we
have done wrong, that we know nothing about
it; that some one else must have done it.
There is nothing so mean as this. Boys love
to think that they are almost men ; but there

is nothing more unmanly than to suffer any boy to be blamed for what you have done, and perhaps to be punished for it. It is bad enough to do wrong, but it makes it twice as bad not to confess it, and perhaps cause some one else to suffer the punishment.

Then there is another little fox, and the last one which I shall mention. He is a cousin or some near relation to Mr. Deceit. His name is Evil-speaking. He destroys much good and makes a great deal of trouble in the world. He puts neighbor against neighbor, and friend against friend. And this destroys our peace and comfort. We speak evil about others, and others speak evil things to us about our friends, and it makes us distrust them, even when we have reason to know that we did not hear the truth; and we cannot be so kind to them as we otherwise would, and cannot love them as much. You see how this prevents the vine which Christ has planted in our hearts from bearing fruit.

Now, children, with these little foxes in your hearts, you can neither become very good, nor do much good. If you look into your hearts, you will all find some of them there, and perhaps others which I have not mentioned. I have told you where the foxes are to be found, and how you may know them. Now I will tell you

II. How to catch them, and kill them.

It is very wicked indeed to take away the life of any thing which God has made, unless it is good for food, or is a destructive animal.

I once saw the picture of a little girl, with a dead bird in her hand. She was showing it to her mother as if she wondered why it would not open its eyes and sing as it used to. And her mother seemed to be telling her that the life was gone; that no one could make it live again but God. He only can give life, and it is wicked for us, without some good cause, to take away the life He has given, from even the meanest of His creatures.

But it is perfectly proper to kill those animals which would take away our lives if they had a chance, or which would destroy the labor of the husbandman. And for this reason it is perfectly proper to kill the foxes, even the little foxes. They look quite innocent when they are small, but they are of the same nature as the great foxes. They will soon grow to be quite as cunning, and their teeth quite as sharp.

But it is very hard to catch the kind of foxes of which I have been speaking; they are so cunning. Indeed, you cannot do it yourselves. Nor does Christ ask you; He says, *Take us the foxes.* That is as if He had said, You and I will go together and catch these foxes. He will help you. He is ready to help you by night or by day.

The first thing necessary to catch them is watchfulness. Be always on the look-out for them. Do not think that they will never come, or that it will only be when you have grown up and gone into the world to meet its temptations. They are in your hearts now, and you must watch for the very first manifestation, or they will become too mighty for you. Little sins soon become great sins. Remember that many a boy has been ruined, both for time and eternity, by reading just one improper book. It let loose a whole train of evil thoughts in his mind, which grew stronger and stronger, till he ran in the ways of evil with greedy feet. O children, *watch* those evil thoughts which rise in your hearts, and cry at once to Christ, Come dear Saviour, and help me to take the foxes, the little foxes, ere they spoil the vines.

The next thing you have to do, to catch and kill the foxes, is *to pray. Pray at all times.* It is not enough to ask God when you retire at night, to forgive you your sins, and when you rise in the morning, for Him to watch over you through the day and keep you from evil. You must learn to "pray without ceasing." When an angry thought rises in your heart, when a sharp and cruel word, which would wound the heart of a companion, comes to your lips, just breathe a silent prayer to Christ to take away the wicked thought and give you grace to withhold the cruel word, and soon you will have no cause to fear these foxes.

When children once learn to pray in this manner, I have no fear for them. At home, or abroad, under the eye of their parents, or away from their control, they will be able to resist evil. The tender vines will not be destroyed, but will soon bring forth rich clusters of grapes.

Think then of these words as the words of Christ addressed to you. Become plants in His vineyard, and let not the foxes destroy the vines, when He is saying to you, "Take us the foxes, the little foxes, that spoil the vines; for our vines have tender grapes."

How to Pray.

LUKE xi. 1. " Lord, teach us to pray."

ON a cold wintry day, a little pale-faced girl stood shivering at the door of a great house in the city. Many people passed by, but no one seemed to notice her, although she looked sad, indeed, for big tears stood in her bright blue eyes. She was a sweet, and timid child, not always poor. She could look back to the time when she had a pleasant home—when she did not know what it was to feel either cold or hunger. She had a good, kind father, and loving brothers and sisters.

But a sad day came—every one in the house moved about just as still as they could,

and when they had occasion to speak, it was
only in a faint whisper. At last, the children
were all called into their father's room. He
lay upon his bed, his cheeks pale and wasted,
and his eyes already beginning to look glassy.
With a great effort he put out his thin hand,
and placing it upon the head of each one of
his children, in turn, implored a blessing upon
them, and then telling them to be good, and
meet him in that bright world to which he
was going, he closed his eyes, and with one
long-drawn sigh, his spirit left the body. He
was dead.

A few days after this, the widowed mother,
and fatherless children, together with a few
kind friends, followed him to the village,
which was his native place, and laid him in
the grave to sleep his last sleep.

After they returned to their city home,
they found to their sorrow, that they were *no
longer* rich, but poor; indeed so poor that
they must leave their present abode, and go
out into the world, to earn their bread by
their own labor. I will not tell you how
sickness entered their humble home, how one

after another, the children were called away
to join their father, till at last the poor mother,
worn out by sorrow and suffering, was laid
upon a sick and dying bed. Then the little
girl was forced to go out and seek relief for
her mother.

It was this that had taken her out that cold
day, and she was trying to find courage to
ring, and make known her wants, at the great
house where we left her standing. Again and
again does she put her hand to the bell, and
take it away without ringing. But as she
stands and hesitates, the door opens, and a
lady with a beautiful little girl, warmly and
richly clad, comes out and looks kindly upon
the poor shivering child. Their hearts are
moved by her look of suffering, so they kindly
take her into their warm home, and listen to
her tale of sorrow. I wish I could tell you
how she begs for her poor sick mother, forgetful of her own hunger. Her looks as well as
her words are imploring. She gains confidence by the kindness shown to her, and as
they bestow upon her something to relieve her
mother's wants, could you have heard her ex-

pressions of gratitude, I am sure you would have done just what the kind lady and her child did—weep.

My object in telling you this story, is to show you what *prayer is.* That little girl prayed. The story she told of her mother's wants and sufferings, and her appeal for help, was her prayer. She asked for what she wanted very much, and she asked it very earnestly. Only she asked from a creature like herself, whereas, when we pray, we pray to God. But we will leave the little girl now to go home with a happy heart to her sick mother, while I tell you three things about the text:

I. To whom we should pray.

II. How we should pray.

III. For what we should pray.

First, then, I am to tell you to whom we are to pray.

Do you know, children, that we are all very poor; indeed, so poor, that we have nothing which we can call our own? The clothes you wear, the food you eat, the air you breathe, is not yours. They have only been lent you for a little while by the good God who made you, and who still keeps you in being.

You would think that a very naughty, wicked child, who should receive, day by day, many good things from its kind parents, and yet should never once say, Thank you, father, thank you, mother, but take them just as if it deserved them, and had a right to them. Yet this is just the way that many children, and I am sorry to say, grown-up people, live. They do not see God, and therefore they never think of Him, and never thank Him for what He gives them. I hope there is no one so wicked here. I should be afraid to live in the same house with such a man or such a child. For God is angry with such people every day. It is only because He is so kind, that He does not take away from them all the good things He has given them.

James and John were brothers. Their father had occasion to go abroad to a distant land to be absent some years. There was a large and beautiful portrait of their father in the palor, which James loved to look at very much, because it made him remember his father. But John never liked to go into that room at all, and when he did, would not cast even a glance at his father's portrait. Almost every month the two brothers received rich and costly presents, just alike. As soon as they were received, James would sit down and write his father a long letter, thanking him for his present, and telling how he remembered him, and longed for his return. But John never took the trouble to write, and when asked by his brother to do so, would answer, " What is the use ? I receive just as many presents as you do, without all this trouble."

At last the father returned, and sent for his two sons. Then he told them to bring the presents which he had sent them, which they did. Opening his trunk, he added to those which James already had, many others more beautiful still. But to John he said, " My son, I have brought nothing home for you, nor are these any longer yours. You were not grateful for all my kindness, and I cannot give such gifts to an ungrateful son." Do you not say it served him right, the ungrateful boy ?

But, children, there are a great many, both old and young, who act like this ungrateful boy toward their heavenly Father. All that they have, they received from Him, and yet have never once thanked Him for it.

This is one reason why we should pray to God, and this is one part of prayer—thanksgiving—returning thanks for what He has given us. If you have kind parents, God has given you them. If you have a happy, pleasant home, God has given you that, also. If you have food and clothing, and all the comforts of life, God has given you these. Have you not then great reason to say, " Thanks be unto God for all the benefits He hath bestowed upon us?"

But another reason why we should pray to God, is, He only can supply your wants.

Had the little girl of whom I told you, gone to some one as poor as herself, she could not have received any relief. They might have wept with her, and expressed their sorrow, but this would have been all they could have done. And thus is it with us. Your parents cannot of themselves provide you with food. It all comes from God.

Many years ago, in the land of Judea, because of the wickedness of the people, God said to them by his prophet, "There shall be no rain for the space of three years and six months." Day after day the sun journeyed through a cloudless sky. Instead of cool breezes springing up in the evening, it was the warm winds of the great desert which swept over the land. The grass in the fields withered, the leaves dropped off the trees, although it was summer, and there was a great famine throughout all the land.

One day, when the sun was very hot, an old man with tottering steps, was seen approaching a humble little hut, where dwelt a poor widow and her only son. While he stood by the door, before knocking, he heard the widow say to her son, "There is only meal enough left to make one little cake; we will bake it, and then lie down together and die."

The prophet, however, knocked at the door,

and the pious widow welcomed him in the name of the Lord.

He then told her that he was faint from hunger and his long journey, and asked for something to eat. She had a kind heart, and would gladly have assisted the prophet, but alas! she had to tell him her circumstances.

Never fear, said the prophet, make me a cake, the Lord will provide. She did so, and what was her surprise, when day after day she continued to bake from the little meal, and it never grew less, till at last the rain came and there was abundance of bread in the land.

Who was it that multiplied the widow's meal? Why God, to be sure. No one else could have done it. Well, this is the way that God provides for us.

It is almost spring. In a few weeks you will see the farmer turning up the rich furrows, and casting in the seed. One bag of grain will plant a large field. But when harvest comes, for this bag of corn he will carry home wagon load after wagon load. Who makes it increase so? Why God—He sends the rain, the dew, and the sunshine. This is the way He feeds us every year. How right and proper is it, then, to pray to him, " Give us this day our daily bread."

But another reason why we should pray to God, is, He always hears our prayers.

Could I take you with me to-day away over the seas, to that great country called China, we would see many strange looking people, and curious looking houses. Could we enter one of these houses, we would find a queer looking little image, made of wood, or iron, or brass, and see not only children, but men and women bowing down before it, and praying to it, just as if it could hear, and give them what they prayed for. But in this happy land, we know better than that. "It has eyes, but it sees not, ears, but it hears not, hands, but it cannot handle, feet, but it cannot walk." And we know too, that God, the living God, can hear us when we cry to Him. Let me illustrate this, by telling you a story.

There was a good little girl once who strayed away into the woods to gather flowers. On she went with tripping footsteps, plucking flowers, as she said to herself, for dear mama, till she grew weary and thought it was time to return home. But, alas, she had lost her way, and instead of going toward home, went farther and farther from it. Then she called for her mother as loud as her little voice could, but there was no one who heard her feeble cry. Foot-sore and weary, and withal very much frightened, for it was now getting to be quite dark, she sat down under a tree, and cried. As she felt like going to sleep, she remembered what her good mother had taught her, about God being ever near and ready to hear us when we pray ; so she knelt down upon the cold ground, and prayed God to watch over her, and take her home to her mother. This was simple and child-like, but it is just the way God loves to have us feel.

Alarmed at home, because their daughter did not return, they began to search for her in the woods, and God directed them to where the little girl was. They found her sleeping sweetly under a tree, with a beautiful smile upon her face. Taking her gently up in their arms, they carried her safely home. When

she awoke, looking around her rather sur-
prised for a moment, she said, "Mother, I
knew He would; I asked God to take me
home, and He heard me, and has."

Don't you think the little girl was right.
Her mother could not hear her feeble cry, but
the great God who has said that he is near to
all who call upon Him, heard her and guided
those who were searching for her to the very
spot where she was.

Yes, children, God can hear us when we
pray. He is not far from each one of us.
And this is another reason why we should
pray to Him.

Some years ago a company of men sailed
from England in a good strong ship, to try
and find what is called the Northwest Passage. To do this, they must sail far away to
the North, where perpetual snow covers the
earth, and the waters are frozen into great
mountains of ice. They expected to be gone
some years, and went provided for this. But
nothing was heard of them for some time, and
people became very anxious for their safety.
They knew that their provisions must be ex-

hausted, and that it would take months to
reach them. You see, their friends, although
they had the heart to help them, were so far
off that they could not reach them in time.
They perished in the arctic snows, but how or
where those brave men died, will never be
known till the people of all lands and nations
meet around the great White Throne. Children, if you live to be men and women, you
may some time be in sore distress, and have
no earthly friend near. But never forget that
God is always near, and that you can cry to
Him, and He can deliver you out of all your
distresses. Let me here tell you how a little
boy reminded his mother of this.

He was the son of a good man, a minister
of the Gospel, but his father died and left
them in destitute circumstances. One day
his mother was very much cast down. Their
money was all gone, and she did not know
how she would be able to provide bread for
her little boy and herself. As she thought of
this, and the dark future came before her
mind, she sat down and wept. For some
time the little boy stood looking anxiously at

his mother. At last he drew near, and putting his little hand in hers, said, "*Mother, is God dead?*" " No, no, my son," she answered, "I had almost forgotten that your father was His servant. He will take care of us, for He has promised to provide for all those who put their trust in Him." And God did provide for them. He raised up kind friends for the widow and her son, and they never knew what want was. It is thus that God is nigh to all them that call upon Him. To whom then should we pray but to God? Now we have come to the second thing I was to tell you.

2. How we are to pray.

A great many years ago some wicked people rebelled against their king, and said that they would no longer obey his laws. The king, although kind and good, said they must be punished, for the laws which they had disobeyed were for the good of all. The punishment was death. They were doomed to die. And now they were right sorry for their wickedness, and said, " Oh, if some one could be found who would plead for us, the king might

spare our lives.   But who would go for them?
They were afraid to go themselves to the king,
because they knew that he was angry with
them.   At length some one said, " If we could
only get the king's son to go for us, the king
loves him so much, and has just made procla-
mation that whatever he asks shall be granted
to him."   So they sent for the king's son, and
told him their sad tale, and how sorry they
were for what they had done.   Upon their
bended knees, they besought him to go and
beseech the king to pardon them.   His heart
was moved to pity, and he went to his father,
and asked him for *his sake* to pardon those
men condemned to death.   The father not
only heard him patiently, but also said,
" There is their pardon; go and take them
out of prison."   With a joyful heart, he
hastened to the prison, knocked off their
heavy chains, and told them to depart, and
sin no more.

Now, children, you and I are like these
poor prisoners.   God is our King.   When we
sin, we break His law.   We were condemned
to die.   And God was so angry with us that

we dared not even ask him to forgive us. But Christ has come, and says to you and me in this good Book, "I will go and intercede for you. I will beseech My Father to pardon you. Yea, My Father, Himself, will hear you, if you will ask in *My name*."

And now, when we pray, it is in Christ's name. We always say in our prayers, for Jesus' sake. Therefore in telling you *how to pray*, this is the first thing: You must pray in the name of Christ; and remember that Christ is with God, the Father, praying for us. But again:

You must pray in faith.

I have sometimes seen a child go to its father or mother, and ask for something it did not expect to get. It either knew that its parents could not or would not grant what it was asking. This was wrong and wicked. And so it is wrong for us to ask God to give us any thing, thinking all the time that He cannot, or *will not* bestow it upon us. I am afraid that this is the way a great many pray. They do not expect to get what they ask for. Children, when you pray you should feel sure

E3

that God can give you every thing you need.
You know every thing is His. There are a
great many things which your parents cannot give you. But God is so rich that He
can give you every thing it is best you should
have.

One cold winter, a few years ago, in the
city of Utica, a minister called upon a poor
family. As he was entering the door he heard
a little child crying, and asking its mother for
bread. But the poor woman, with a sad
heart, had to say, "Hush, my child, I have
no bread to give you."

But when you need any thing as much as
that poor child needed bread, and cry to God
for it, He will never give you such an answer.
He can give you all you need, so you can always ask with confidence, that is, believing
that God is both able and willing to answer
your prayers. But again :

You must not only ask in faith, but you
must also ask in *earnest*, that is, with your
heart.

A child only six years old, said to her Sun-
day school teacher, "When we kneel down in

the school room to pray, it seems as if my *heart talked*." That child had learned how to pray.

So was it with the little girl I told you about, who went to the lady's door, begging. She wanted what she asked for very much indeed. Every word that she spoke, came from the heart.

We may repeat words to God, but that is not prayer, unless we *feel* what we say.

If John should come to me and ask for a book, and I could see by his manner that he did not care at all for the book, but had only come because his mother or some one else had sent him, I don't think I would give him the book, because I should know that if he took it home, he would not read it. But if I should see that he wanted the book very much, and was anxious to read and learn, I would say at once, "John, there's the book, and welcome. Come again when you want another."

Now, this is just the way that God gives the good things which He has; only to those who ask in earnest. If you ask because your parents or Sabbath school teachers told you that you should pray, and not because you feel your need of them, God will not heed your prayers.

This, then, is the way we should pray. In the name of Christ, believing that God can give us what we ask—feeling our need of the things for which we ask, or what is the same, asking with our hearts. And now we come to the last thing that I was to tell you, namely:

3. For what we should pray.

And first we are to pray

(1.) That God would teach us how to pray.

That is the prayer of the text, "Lord teach us to pray." It was one of His disciples who asked Jesus this, and you know that they were ministers. So you see, children, that God has to teach ministers to pray. They cannot pray aright unless He does. And if He has to teach them, He is the only one who can teach you. This, then, is the first thing you are to ask, "Lord, teach me to pray." The second thing is, that

(2.) God would make you sorry for your sins.

We all sin. The great difference between the good and the bad is, that the one are sorry for their sins, while the others are not.

Two little boys were playing together in the garden one day. Upon a little dwarf tree there were some pears which in the sun looked yellow and ripe. Their father had told them that they must not pick those pears; that when they were quite ripe they should have some of them. But the pears looked so tempting that they forgot what their father had said, and each of them put forth his hand and picked one, and ran off into some out of the way place to eat it. It tasted sweet at first, but soon they began to think of what their father had told them. A little voice, too, kept whispering all the time in their hearts, "That was wicked; you have done wrong." And this made the little boys sad.

One of them thought how his father would punish them, when he found it out. The other thought only of his wickedness in disobeying his father. The one said, "I will not tell father; perhaps he will never find it out." But the other said, "I cannot be happy till my father has forgiven me;" and went and told him what he had done. "My son," said the father, "I forgive you, but I must punish you. You must not go out any more to-day, although it is Saturday." And the boy answered, "It is right; you are very kind to forgive me." While his other son concealed from his father what he had done, and did not feel sorry for his disobedience.

We are all like the wicked boy. We do not feel sorry for our sins, and would do them again, and again, if we were not afraid of the punishment. And God only can make us truly sorry for them. He will do it if we ask Him. But again:

(3.) We should pray to have our sins blotted out by the peace-speaking blood of Christ.

We read in the last book in the Bible, that in the Day of Judgment *the books* will be opened. One of these books is called, the Book of God's Remembrance. In that book every sin which you have ever committed is recorded. There they stand against you; and will be read before the whole universe, unless they are blotted out. There is nothing which will take them away but the blood of Christ. When we ask God to forgive us our sins, and He answers our prayer, Christ takes his hand which was pierced by the cruel nails that fixed Him to the cross, and draws it down the page which has your name at the top, and the long list of your sins disappears. After that, there are no sins charged against you. For what the recording angel writes there by day, when you go to God at night, and pray, For Jesus' sake, forgive me the sins of this day, Christ blots them out. So that there will be nothing to condemn you in the Day of Judgment. Happy must they be whose sins are thus forgiven. And it is a blessed truth, children, that they can be forgiven, if we will only ask.

These are only a few of the things for which we should pray. It would make a very long sermon, indeed, if I should try to tell you them all. I have surely told you enough, to have you desire to learn to pray. You are not too young. God hears little children when they pray. When once a child has learned this, it is safe both for this world, and that which is to come. If you know how to pray, you will be shielded from temptation in life; and when life is done, you will enter heaven; for the Christian enters heaven by prayer.

The Glorious Victory.

———◦———

1 Cor. xv. 57. "Thanks be to God, which giveth us the victory."

SOME years ago I attended a grand concert in the city of New York. It was in the old Broadway Tabernacle, which was then one of the largest buildings in the city. The musicians were so numerous that they reminded me of the great choir in Solomon's Temple, which had Asaph for its leader. When they played upon their instruments of music, the sweet harmony rolled through the building like the sound of many waters.

It was a very strange piece they performed that night. The composer would only suffer

them to use it upon the condition that pro-
grammes were presented to the audience with
an explanation. I think it was called a de-
scriptive symphony, and was meant to describe by sound, peace and war, and the rejoicing after the victory.

Having carefully read over the explanation,
I waited rather impatiently to hear how they
could give expression in music to these different scenes. Soon they commenced. The
notes were low and sweet—full of melody;
just like the sounds you hear on a beautiful
summer evening, when the very stars seem to
be singing as they shine, and all nature seems
to be saying, "Praise the Lord, for He is
good; His mercy endureth forever." Then
there seemed to be a change in the key, and
a quicker movement in the time. It was like
the hum of active, but peaceful industry.
You seemed to hear the joyful song of the
laborer who delights in his task, and the song
of the maiden louder than the buzzing of her
spinning wheel.

But by-and-by there seemed to be notes of
alarm, as when the first tidings of some ca-

lamity reaches a place. It was the mingling of hopes and fears in sound. But gradually the notes of fear and sorrow prevailed. War had been declared. The hum of labor was still heard, but there was no cheerful songs mingling with it. You could hear now and then the muster call to arms.

The preparations for departure were now heard. At last the time for parting came. What a blending of sounds did we then hear. Low, tender farewells, which might never be repeated, and great bursts of anguish, which seemed almost to break the heart. Sometimes the sounds seemed to be the inspiration of hope, as if they had lived through the months of separation, and were welcoming them home again. Sometimes it was the expression of foreboding fears, as if they felt that it was a last farewell. The musical instruments under the hands of skillful players almost seemed to speak, and even feel.

Then you could hear the call to march, and the heavy tramp of armed men. Fainter and fainter grew the sounds, till at last it seemed as though they came from a great distance, and then died away. There was a pause.

When they began again it was a perfect chaos of sounds, but gradually they became more harmonious. It was the bustling preparation for battle. Then came the march of a mighty host, under which the very earth, seemed to tremble. Now might be heard the rattle of musketry, and once in a while the booming of a cannon. These volleys became more frequent, and the strokes on the great drum more numerous, till they seemed to be all mingled into horrible din and clamor. The instruments seemed to speak. Here were shouts of victory; yonder, shouts of terror and dismay.

The noise of the cannon and musketry died away, and shrieks and groans were heard in their stead. Slow were the measures and heavy the tramp, as if they were carrying the wounded from the field of battle. Then, the sweet though solemn voices of the night were heard, but it was night on the battle field. The quiet was broken, the harmony disturbed by the sad sound of human distress. There was another pause.

Then came the rejoicing, after the victory; the march toward home, which I will not describe. Then came the meeting. They were back in the quiet homes they had left. There were tender, tearful welcomes, the expressions of joy. Then came the grand "Te Deum," as if all had gone to the great cathedral to return their thanks to God for the victory. But now and then the ear would catch a note so sad that the tears would come unbidden to the eyes. It seemed to express a widow's or a maiden's anguish, whose husband or lover had been left dead on the distant battle field. These sorrowful notes told of the great expense at which the victory had been won.

It was a wonderful composition, and a wonderful performance.

I know that you are all wondering why I should tell you about that concert, for it can have nothing at all to do with the text. I wondered myself why this passage of Scripture should have brought it to my mind, for I had not thought of it before in some years.

Let us read the text again, and see if we can
find out the connection: "Thanks be unto
God, who giveth us the *victory.*" Ah, yes,
the last word is the key to the whole—*the victory.*

Do you see now why I thought of that long
forgotten circumstance? No? Well, I must
try and tell you.

In thinking of the victory spoken of in my
text, I thought of other victories, and how
there was always sorrow as well as rejoicing,
connected with them. And then I thought,
what a glorious victory this must be when *all*
can join in saying, "Thanks be unto God,
who giveth us the victory." No orphans to
mourn the loss of a father. No father and
mother to mourn the loss of a brave son. No
soldier to mourn the loss of a comrade, who
perhaps fell dead while fighting at his side.
All rejoice, but none are sad, because of this
victory. It is a victory in which I hope you
all will share a part.

You know, children, that a victory is getting the better of an enemy. You cannot get
a victory unless there is some enemy to over-

come; so although this sermon is to be about "The Glorious Victory," I will have to tell you first

I. The foes we have to conquer.

You know that the text is to be found almost at the end of one of the longest chapters in the New Testament. It was Paul who wrote this part of the Bible, and this chapter is one of the most sublime in the whole book. I will tell you why: There are things in it which you can find no where else.

I have been in large buildings, the walls of which were all covered with books. On this side were books which were written hundreds of years ago; and on that, books written long before. There were the works of Plato, and Socrates, and Homer, in Greek; of Virgil, and Cicero, and Cæsar, in Latin, and a host of other men's works, who were considered very wise. But all these books together were not worth this one chapter. With all their wisdom, they did not know how Death was to be conquered—how the Grave was to give back all the treasures which had been laid there.

Why, would you believe it, children, some

of these wise men looked for a spring, the
waters of which would make them immortal.
They climbed high mountains to see if it was
not hid upon their tops; they explored broad
valleys and sandy dererts, trying to find it.
But when they came back from their wan-
derings, they had to say, We have not found
it.

Others said that the juice of some plants
would make them live forever. And so they
collected plants and herbs; they shut themselves up in secret places, to extract the juice.
But all their labor did not profit. Their
friends died—they died. They had not heard
of the gracious Saviour, who said of Himself,
"I am the water of life; I am the balm of
Gilead." They knew nothing of all this.

But this chapter tells us how Death is to
be conquered, and how the dead are to come
forth out of their graves. Do you know how
dark the grave looked when you saw your
mother or father, your baby brother, or little
sister, laid there. O, it seemed so cruel to
cover them up in the cold, damp ground, so
that you could see them no more. You hate

to think that before long, you, too, must die, and be put there. And it would be all darkness, all sorrow, if we had not this blessed book. We would ask, Shall I ever see these dear ones again? and receive no answer.

Said a little girl to a minister, who found her weeping by her mother's grave, "O, sir, will mother never come back to me; she has been so long away? I know she is here, for I saw them put her down there; but although I come and call her every day, she does not answer me."

Now, what do you think the good man told her? "My child," said he, "your mother must sleep there a great many years. You cannot awake her, but by-and-by, Jesus will call· both you and her, and you will come forth in beautiful garments from the tomb."

How did he know this? Why, he had read this chapter. It tells us that all the generations of the past are to rise from the dead —the young and the old, the rich and the poor. They will hear the voice of the "Son of Man;" and Death, the great enemy which took them away and hid them in the grave, thinking to keep them there forever, must let them go, and they shall come forth, to die no more. Death is the great enemy over which we are to gain the victory.

But I see you are wondering how we are going to conquer Death, since Death first conquers us all. The youngest of you know that when he comes into our homes, we cannot resist him. If he lay his hand upon the little babe on its mother's breast, a mother's tears and entreaties will not allure him from his purpose. If he lay his hand on a kind father or a loving mother, the children may pray, but he heeds them not—the father or mother must go. Thus we have to live in fear, not knowing when he will come for us. It is true, children, that he is a mighty destroyer. He commenced with the pious Abel, and he has reigned till the present. He took all the prophets and apostles. He slew David, who conquered the great giant; and all the great and mighty ones of the past. Soon we, too, must fall under his power.

Now, can you tell me how Death came into this world? Was it not by sin? You

know what God said to Aoam in Eden : "In
the day thou eatest thereof thou shait surely
die." Just as soon as he broke God's command—for that is sin—he began to die. And
it is just for the same reason that we must
die. We all have sinned. If we can only
conquer sin, we shall gain a victory over
Death. Let me see if I can make this plain
by telling you two stories, which you will all
be able to understand.

There was once a rich man, who lived in a
very fine house, which was his pride and the
admiration of all who beheld it. It was not
situated upon the wayside, like most houses.
You had to go up a long avenue, shaded with
beautiful trees, to reach it. And what a
charming spot it was. Around the house was
a fine garden, in which were flowers both rich
and rare. Here and there were fountains of
water, which shot up in crystal streams and
fell in misty showers. Within, there was
every thing that could please and delight. It
was a splendid home. Many a one envied its
possessor. But now I wish you to come with
me and see the owner of this beautiful man-

sion.   You know we can in imagination, even enter into the king's palace, so in the same way, no bolts or bars can keep us out of the rich man's dwelling. We will pass by all these richly-furnished rooms. We will not even pause to look at those rich pictures in the gallery. We will go into his chamber, and see the rich man himself.

There he is, upon his bed, for he is sick, even unto death. I know that it is hard to look upon the sick and suffering, and more especially when they have no hope in Christ. He has every thing to make him comfortable, but his eye seems to be fixed in anxious expectation upon the door, as if he was looking for some one to enter. It is his faithful pastor who has come, and the dying man says to him, " O, sir, I cannot die; *I cannot die.* I have no hope for the future; what must I do to be saved?" The good man tells him of the Saviour, who died for him, and who has taken away the sting of Death—a Saviour whose blood cleanseth from all sin ; and then urges him to go to Christ, as *his* Saviour. But the dying man answers, "It is too late. I have

spent my life in sin and folly. _ have blas-
phemed the name of Jesus. I have oppressed
the poor, and taken advantage of the needy.
I am lost! I am lost! there is no hope for me.
Death is coming; O for another day—another
hour." But it could not be. He had given
himself to sin in his life, and now Death
gains the victory over him. *The sting of
Death is sin.*

But now come with me from the country to
the city. We must leave the green fields and
the flowers behind us. It is a short walk by
night that I wish you to take with me, but
not through the crowded streets where the
light from so many windows makes it almost
as bright as day. Do you see that little dark
alley, so damp and dark that the few lights
seem afraid to shine. Do not fear, although
you hear the sounds of horrid revelry. It is
a wicked spot. Keep close to me and no evil
shall befall you as we go up these crazy steps.
Another flight, another flight, and yet another. Here is the room to which I would
conduct you. What a gloomy place. No
fire on the hearth, although it is bitter cold,

and only one sickly light, which hardly re-
lieves the darkness. Hark! do you not hear
music almost as sweet as the song of the angels? Look around, and see if you can dis-
cover whence it comes. See, something
moves in yonder corner. Let us see what it
is. There is only a bundle of straw and a
thin, ragged cover. Hold down the light.
See that face—the traces of suffering are still
upon it. The little sufferer has known want.
He, too, like the rich man, is dying. His
eyes are closed, but a sweet smile flits across
his countenance, just like the playing of a
sunbeam upon a marble statue. His dreams
must be pleasant. Shall we awake him?
Speak his name softly—" Johnny! Johnny!"
His eyes open—large, deep blue eyes. "Why
did you smile so sweetly in your sleep, Johnny?" "O, sir, I had such a beautiful dream,
and I thought it was not all a dream.

"I thought I saw a beautiful city. It was
all shining with light, and yet there was no
sun. There were a great many people in its
streets, but they all looked so happy. They
had white robes, and harps in their hands.

But what made me feel so happy was, that I thought I heard the Saviour say, 'Go, and bring Johnny home'—and you awoke me just as they were coming."

Shall I tell the poor boy that he is dying? "Johnny, do you know that you have only a few hours to live?" "O, yes, sir," he answers, "but I am not afraid to die. Just raise up my head a little, if you please. Thank you, sir, that will do." "Why are you not afraid to die?" "Jesus has died for me, sir." "Where did you learn that?" "In the Sabbath school, sir. Please sing to me that beautiful hymn, 'We're homeward bound'"—and as we sing he says, "They're coming; they're coming; I knew it was not a dream. Good-by, sir; I'm going home." And little Johnny was dead.

I believe that all he saw was just as real as the vision which Stephen, the first martyr, had.

Both of these stories are true, children. I have told them to you in my own words, but they are what happens every day. Some die happy, like little Johnny, and some die in

fearful agony, like the rich man.   Shall I tell
you what makes the difference?   Some have
Christ for their Saviour; their sins have been
washed away with His blood, and to them,
dying is but going home, to be forever with
the Lord.   While others reject Christ, and so
Death comes as an enemy, and in the fearful
strife he is the conqueror; they feel his dart
and sting just as keenly as if Christ had not
died.

Now, then, if you would gain the victory
over Death, you must, while you have health
and strength, in the days of your youth, go to
Jesus, and choose Him for your Saviour.
Then, should you live to old age, or die in
youth, you will be able to say, with your last
breath, "Thanks be unto God, who giveth us
the victory."

But now I must tell you, in the second
place, about

II. The song which the victors sing.

I have told you of the great rejoicing there
is when a nation has gained a great victory.

When the children of Israel passed through
the Red Sea, and their enemies attempting to

follow them, perished in the water, Miriam,
the sister of Moses, led the congregation of
Israel in a song of rejoicing—thanking God
for the great overthrow of their enemies.
None of the Israelites were lost in the sea ;
none of them had to mourn while the others
were rejoicing, because the victory had cost
them some near and dear friend. The victor's
song that we would speak about, is one of the
same kind. There was a time when only one
in heaven could sing that song, for strange as
it may seem to you, children, angels and archangels cannot join in it. When the redeemed
begin to sing the song of salvation, all the rest
in heaven pause to listen.

But I was saying there was a time when
only one in heaven could sing the victor's
song—that was Abel. He stooped solitary
and alone before the throne to sing of redeeming love. But others, and others, and others,
were added, and now it is a great company,
which no man can number, who make the
high vault of heaven ring, as they raise their
voices, saying—for this is the victor's song—
" Worthy is the Lamb, which was slain, to re-

ceive power, and riches, and glory, for He
hath redeemed us with His blood, and made
us kings and priests to our God."

O it is a sweet song.   Let me ask you, children, shall you and I sing that song together,
before the throne of God?

But now let me tell you in the last place

III. What robes the victors shall wear.

When I was in Canada, some years ago, I
noticed a great many soldiers there, and the
most of them displayed a silver medal, attach-
ed to a blue ribbon.   They seemed to be very
proud of that badge, and the people, too,
seemed to be proud to have such soldiers
among them.

I asked one of them why he and his companions wore the medals, and he answered
me thus: "We have been in the Crimean
war, sir, and the Sultan of Turkey has given
us this as a mark of his appreciation of our
services."   It was the badge of a victor.

But how shall I describe to you the badge
which the heavenly conquerors wear?   I could
not tell you any thing about it had I not read
of a man who was permitted to behold these

victors in the glorious garments which they wear. He tell us that they are clothed in *white robes*, and have palms of victory in their hands. Crowns, too, are upon their brows, for they are kings as well as conquerors. Some of these crowns are weighty with jewels of priceless value. For those who have turned many to righteousness, have jeweled crowns given unto them. For every soul they saved there is a jewel, which sparkles like a star of the first magnitude.

Now, children, would you be one of these glorious victors; thus to reign and live with Christ? Then you must begin now, to fight the good fight of faith. Then we shall soon enter that city, and join in that worship where

> " Sweetest strains, from soft harps stealing,
> Trumpet notes, of trumpets pealing,
> Radiant wings and white stoles gleaming,
> Up the steps of glory streaming,
> Where the heavenly bells are ringing
> Holy, holy, holy! singing
>   To the mighty Trinity;
> Holy, holy, holy, crying,
> For all earthly care and sighing,
>   In that city cease to be."

The Parting Promise.

———•———

JOHN xiv. 2–4. "I go to prepare a place for you, and if I go and prepare a place for you, I will come again and receive you unto Myself, that where I am there ye may be also ; and *whither I go ye know, and the way ye know.*"

I WISH, children, to take a long journey with you to-day; that is, if you would like to go with me so far from home. It is one of those journeys which we can take, and yet never leave our places. I am not a very old man yet, and still I have been all over the world. I have stood on Mount Sinai, where God once came down to give His law to the children of Israel, and have looked upon the great waste, howling wilderness all around. I have journeyed through the desert, and walked up Mount Nebo, from which Moses saw the Land of Promise. I have seen the Jordan, and the place where Jericho once stood. I have walked all over that pleasant land, its green valleys and vine-clad hills. I have seen the palace of Solomon, whose magnificence the Queen of Sheba admired so much, and the beautiful temple, which from porch to altar was one blaze of splendor. I have walked with Christ to Bethany, and come back with Him, too, over the Mount of Olives. I have been with Him in the gloomy garden of Gethsemane and in the judgment hall of Pilate. I have walked with Him through the streets of Jerusalem when He was going to Calvary to be crucified. I have stood beside His cross, and have seen the cruel soldiers driving the nails into His hands and feet, and I have watched there till He bowed His head, saying, "It is finished." Why, children, I have been over all the world, but I will not tell you about my travels to-day. I have learned a secret, and I will tell it to you, for once in a while I like

company in my travels. You have all read
Fairy Tales: those strange little creatures
you read about seem to have the power (that
is, if you believe the stories) of being just
where they want to be. I have learned how
they do it. It is by the imagination. When
you read a book of travels, just try and think
that you really see the places described, and
it is almost the same thing as being there.
This is the way I do most of my travelling;
just imagine myself where I want to be. It
is a journey like this, that I wish you to take
with me to-day. We will cross the ocean, for
there is something there I would like you to
see.

Now, are you all ready to go ? Well, here
we are in New York already. We have not
time to look at any thing, so we will go on.
Here is a good ship that will answer our purpose. We are all on board. The sails are
unfurled, and away we go. The land is lost
to view already. It is the great ocean that
is all around us. A beautiful day on the
ocean ; nothing but a gentle swell, which you
hardly feel. Here and there you can see a

white sail, or the smoke from one of those great ships which waits neither for winds nor waves. It is blue sky above; blue water beneath But do you see those white cliffs? That is the shore of England, and we are almost at our journey's end. Here we are on British soil at last. We will go away now, over the mountains and glens, and we will stop at that little cottage there. Do you see it, almost covered with honeysuckles?—a sweet little home. I am sure we will find a pleasant family within. An Englishman calls his home his castle; the Queen herself has no right to enter without knocking, but we will go in at once, for we are privileged characters. There is the father and mother and six little ones, but they all look sad. I wonder what is the matter; well, let us listen—they will tell their own story. The father is speaking: " Yes," he says, " yes, children, I must go and seek a new home for you, and when it is all prepared, I will either come again, or send some one for you, and then we will all be so happy again, in our *new home*." Do you wonder that the children should cry, and

that they should ask so anxiously, " But where
are you going, father?"   It is not at all
strange—it would be if it were otherwise—
and he tells them that he is going across the
ocean, to America; a strange, far-off land,
which they have never seen.   And now for a
few weeks they are all busy, making preparations for father's departure; and the day of
separation comes too soon.   We will go with
them to the ship : how tenderly does he bid
them adieu, and what words of comfort does
he speak, trying to hide the big tears which
will come into his eyes, whether or no.   " It
is only for a little while, children ; you know
where I am going, and you know the way,
for we have talked it all over.   I would not
leave you, but it is necessary that I should go
away.   Think of me when I am gone, read
the letters I send you, and be always ready,
so that you may come when I send for you;
farewell, farewell till then."   And now he
steps upon the ship; it is already moving ;
and we will go with him, for I do not wish
any of you left in a strange land.   See them
watching there on the shore, and waving their

adieus as long as they can see their father.
And oh how wistfully he looks back, as the
land recedes from view, till at last it appears
only like a cloud on the horizon. Well, it is
sometimes a long passage to cross the ocean
in a sailing vessel; sometimes the wind dies
away so that the ocean is almost like a great
mirror; sometimes it blows a perfect gale, so
that they have to reef the sails, and then the
ship reels and staggers like a drunken man—
tossed on the summit of this wave, and now
on that; then the wind blows from the wrong
quarter, and they have to sail this way and
that, going several miles to advance one
towards their desired haven; but you can see
that in fair weather or foul, that father is ever
thinking of the loved ones he left behind.
All rejoice when they hear the cry of "Land,
Ho!" but none more than the man who has
gone to find a home for his children. And
now we are back once more at New York,
and our fellow passenger with us. Well, we
will follow him now. He has heard of the
far-famed prairies of the West, where the land
is rich and to be had almost for the asking,

:and hither he directs his steps. Here is land
:for sale, and here he makes his purchase. Dil-
:igently he goes to work breaking up the soil,
which had remained undisturbed since the
morning of creation, and then he begins to
build a home—a home for his wife and children. Months pass away. They have heard
often from him, and he has heard from them.
At last he writes telling them to come, that
the new home is ready for them; he cannot
come after them, but they know the way, for
he has told them all about it, and he will
meet them just as soon as they land, to conduct them to their new home. What a joyful letter that is for those children—they had
never called the old cottage home since father left, but every day spoke about their new
home which father had gone to prepare. It
is hard for them to bid their neighbors and
friends farewell, but this pain of parting is almost forgotten in the great joy of being so
soon with their father. They stand now on
the deck of the vessel, they see the land growing more and more indistinct; they fear as
they see the blue, cold water all around them,

but they forget their fears as they remember that they are going home. And who can describe their joy when all dangers are past, as they meet their dear father in the new land. What a happy night is the first they spend in their new home. And how it adds to their happiness to be told by their father, "Dear children, we will never have to leave this home; it is ours, and no man can take it from us. Have I not fulfilled the promise I made you when I left you, that I would send for you; that where I am, there ye may be also?"

Well, children, are we not getting to be famous travellers? We have been to England and back again twice, all in about ten minutes, and you have not even left your places. But I know you are all wondering what this has to do with my text, and how I am going to make it part of a sermon. Let us read the text again: "I go to prepare a place for you, and if I go and prepare a place for you, I will come again and receive you to Myself, that where I am, there ye may be also, and whither I go ye know, and the way ye know." Well,

I have told you all this to try and illustrate my text. I know, if you have paid attention, that you understand all I said about that father and his family. He went away to prepare a home for his children, and then he sent for them. You know how precious such a promise would be to you, if you were one of the children of that family; and yet my text is a far more precious promise, and a promise for you and for me, if we will only make it ours.

Yes, children, it is a promise which has been fulfilled to more than one since I last preached to you, who are not here to day and never will be. You know that there is a vacant place in the Sabbath school, a seat in one class empty. Some months ago, a message from Christ came into a family, and said to one of their number, " Be ready, I am coming to take you to the home which I have prepared." And we tried, by reading the letter which Christ sent to her about the way, to help her in making her preparations. And then we told her about the beautiful home to which she was going, and tried to calm her fears, till we had to bid her adieu, as she

went forth on that ocean where we could not
follow; that ocean which washes the shores of
eternity.

Do you understand me, children? The messenger which Christ sent was sickness; the
stormy ocean which we can only pass over
once, and that, too, all alone, so far as human
friends are concerned, was death, and we have
a good hope that to-day, while we are still
here, she is in that glorious home with Christ;
or in other words, that this promise in our
text has been fulfilled, "I will come again
and receive you unto Myself, and where I am
there ye may be also."

Now, if the remembrance of this will not
make you serious and thoughtful, I know not
what will. I might tell you a thousand times
that you must die, and yet it might make but
little impression upon you. You might say,
"I am young; death is far off; time enough
to prepare for that;" but now what can you
answer, when death has come into your own
circle, and taken one as young as you all?
Just ask yourself, "*Had it been I*, could I have
felt this sweet text mine, and that I was go-

ing to be forever with the Saviour?" And what is the answer that your own heart gives to the solemn question? Oh how I wish you would all try and answer that question, for I do begin to fear that some of you may live and die without coming to the Saviour. Now remember that I am not here to-day to amuse you, or merely to instruct you. I come to-day as a *messenger* sent from Christ, to tell you of that other messenger who is coming, and to entreat you to be prepared for his coming. I am sent to tell you how the promise may be yours, and to induce you, if possible, to begin this very day to prepare for heaven. Now, that you may understand this text fully, I will first tell you

I. When and by whom these words were spoken.

II. Where Christ was going.

III. How He fulfilled the promise.

IV. How you may make it yours.

First, then, I am to tell you who spake these words, and when they were spoken.

Go with me now, children, to Jerusalem, that beautiful city which for many years was

the joy o. the whole earth. We will enter
this lowly dwelling, for here is the guest
chamber where Christ has gone to eat the
Passover with His disciples. There is Christ
Himself at the table, and John, the disciple
whom Jesus loved, leaning on His breast.
One of the disciples is not here—Judas has
gone out to betray his Lord for thirty pieces
of silver. Do you not see that they are all
looking very sad, just as men do when they
have heard bad news? Do you ask what is
the matter? Christ has just told them that
He was going away to leave them, and they
are very sorrowful, for they did love Christ,
and it makes them sad to know that they are
to be separated from Him, even for a little
while; and now He begins to comfort them.
Hear how beautifully and touchingly He
speaks: " Let not your hearts be troubled; ye
believe in God, believe also in me; in My
Father's house are many mansions; if it were
not so, I would have told you; I go to prepare
a place for you, and if I go away, I will come
again, and receive you unto Myself, that
where I am, there ye may be also." You see

r4

it is just like the way that father talked to
his children; almost the very same language.
Now you know, children, what followed on
the morrow. Christ was crucified. Before
another day was ended, He hung lifeless upon
the accursed tree. But He knew it all, and
He did not fear death. He died that He
might take away the sting of death, that
death instead of being the King of Terrors to
us, might be a messenger whom Christ would
send to take His own people home. Now
was it not kind of Christ to speak so comfort-
ingly to His disciples when His own soul was
sorrowful even unto death? Aye, and He
thought then not merely of the few disciples
who were with Him, but of you and me, if
we are His. And now let me tell you something :

II. Where Christ was going.

For a few Sabbaths I have been preaching
about heaven, and I will tell you why: because so many of our friends have, as we hope,
been called there. I love sometimes to think
over those who expect to meet in heaven.
There are more than one of the Sabbath school

scholars who once belonged to this school,
there. Some of them died so peacefully, so
happy, that it did not seem like dying at all,
and do you know, children, I have a strange
fancy that when I die and the angels come to
take me home, that I will meet them at the
golden gate of the city, and that they will
take me to Jesus, that He may welcome me
to my new home, and that with them I shall
walk through all those shining streets. They
will show me where the river of life is, and
the tree which bears twelve manner of fruits.
They will talk of the instruction they received
in the Sabbath school, and in the Sanctuary
here, and then we will wait together for the
other friends who are coming after us. I
know that they are always happy in heaven,
but I think it is a peculiarly joyful day when
we are weeping here because some friend has
passed away from earth, because they have
met to part no more in heaven. But I am
forgetting I commenced to tell you where
Christ was going—to His own home in heaven.
I preached to you once from the second verse
of this chapter: "In my Father's house are

many mansions." Do you remember it? I
told you then of the golden walls and pearly
gates. I told you of the throne of God, and
of the Lamb. Christ had lived there from all
eternity, and then He came to this earth for
a very few years, and said to His disciples, " I
have finished my work here, now I am going
to My home; do not weep, rather rejoice, for
it is a glorious home; no sin, no sorrow, no
suffering there. I will not forget you, I will
come again and receive you unto Myself, that
where I am, there ye may be also." And now
let me tell you

III. How Christ has fulfilled this promise.

You know that the Apostle John wrote this
part of the Bible, and he lived till all the
other apostles were dead. It seemed almost
as though Christ had forgotten John. He
had sent for Paul, and Peter, Andrew, and
Thomas, and all the rest but John. He heard
about this, and yet no message came for him.
But Christ came to him in a beautiful vision.
The whole of the last book in the Bible is
about it. He saw the Saviour in His home
in glory. He saw Stephen and Simeon—some

of his own children in the Gospel, and all his
fellow laborers there. And I have always
thought that John must have been very im-
patient after that vision to get away from this
world, and yet he did wait patiently till he
was almost a hundred years old, and even
when he was so infirm that he could not walk
to church, he desired to be carried there, when
the only message he could deliver was, " Little children, love one another." But at last
John's time came; he had never thought for
a moment that he was forgotten; and the
promise of Christ was fulfilled to all the apostles. The twelve apostles of the Lamb were
with Him in glory. But do you say, "Ah,
then if the promise has been fulfilled it cannot be for us?" But this is not so. It was
left here for all who would be Christ's disciples, down even to the end of time. So that
it will not be fulfilled till the whole Church of
God are safe in heaven, and we think that
that will be many years hence. But so far as
individuals are concerned, He is fulfilling His
promise every day; for there is not a single
day passes but what He comes and takes some

of His people to be with Himself. Let me tell you how He took a little girl home. She had only been in this world nine short years ; she was a lovely child, and was early prepared for heaven, and then she began to fade away from earth. In her sickness, she said to one of the family, " When I am dead, I wish my pastor might preach a sermon to the children, to persuade them to love Jesus, to obey their parents, and think more about heaven. I have been thinking I should like to have him preach from the text about the prophet Elisha and the child of the Shumanite : ' Is it well with the child, and she answered, It is well.' The prophet will come to see you after I am gone, and when he says, ' How is it with the child?' you may say, ' It is well.' I am sure it will be well with me then, for I shall be in heaven, singing the praises of the Lord." Think you that that child did not feel that the promise was all hers, that Christ was coming to take her to be with Himself? And so many, many more, as young as you are.

And I am now to tell you in the fourth and last place :

IV. How you may make this promise yours.

And *first*, you must get a *title to heaven*. A title to heaven—do you ask what is a title? If your father wished to purchase a house, before he paid the money he would examine the right which the man had to the property— that is, the title; so that he might know whether it really belonged to the man, or not; if he found the title all right, he would then pay the money, and the title would then be transferred to him. Now, you need to get a title to one of the mansions in heaven, before you can say that it is yours; and where, think you, can you get that title? where shall money enough be found to purchase it? You must go to Him who owns heaven and all its glory —and I have glorious news to tell you—*He gives away these titles*, asks nothing for them, but only to come and take them freely. freely, without money and without price. Heaven belongs to Jesus. He purchased it for us with His own blood. And now will you go to Him *to-day?* for He invites you to come, and as- sures you that if you come now, that He will give you what you ask; and where do you think He will write it? upon your heart, so that it can never be lost.

But again, secondly, you must get clean hearts to fit you for heaven. How ashamed you would be to go to some great feast with soiled garments! but you know that heaven is sometimes represented as the marriage supper of the Lamb; and the company are clothed with fine linen, clean and white; for the fine linen is the righteousness of the saints: but our hearts are all defiled by sin. How ashamed we would feel in heaven with our hearts just as they now are! Now we must go to Christ, and have Him cleanse them. His blood was shed for this; and oh it makes the vilest clean. His blood availed for me.

And then, lastly, you must follow the directions which He has given you, and thus be journeying towards heaven, till He meets you on the way. This is His letter to you; read it every day; follow its directions, and so will you be saved from sin and sorrow here, and from eternal misery hereafter.

Now, children, will you do this, so that tho

promise of the text may be yours? You have but a little while to live in the world. Soon death will come, but it will then have no terrors for you : Christ will come and meet you and take you to His home.

www.ingramcontent.com/pod-product-compliance
Lightning Source LLC
Chambersburg PA
CBHW030836270326
41928CB00007B/1073